VISUAL PREFERENCES OF TRAVELERS ALONG THE BLUE RIDGE PARKWAY

VISUAL PREFERENCES OF TRAVELERS ALONG THE BLUE RIDGE PARKWAY

Edited by:
Francis P. Noe
William E. Hammitt

Scientific Monograph Series No. 18

U.S. Department of Interior
National Park Service
Washington, D.C.
1988

As the Nation's principal conservation agency, the Department of the Interior has responsibility for most of our nationally owned public lands and natural resources. This includes fostering the wisest use of our land and water resources, protecting our fish and wildlife, preserving the environment and cultural value of our national parks and historical places, and providing for the enjoyment of life through outdoor recreation. The Department assesses our energy and mineral resources and works to assure that their development is in the best interests of all our people. The Department also has a major responsibility for American Indian reservation communities and for people who live in island territories under U.S. administration.

Library of Congress Cataloging-in-Publication Data

Visual preferences of travelers along the Blue Ridge
  Parkway.

  (Scientific monograph series; no. 18)
  Bibliography: p.
  Includes index.
  Supt. of Docs. no.: I 29.80:18
  1. Blue Ridge Parkway (Va. and N.C.)—Description
and travel. 2. Landscape—Blue Ridge Parkway (Va. and
N.C.). I. Noe, Francis P., 1939-   . II. Hammitt,
William E. III. Series: National Park Service
scientific monograph series; no. 18.
F217.B6V57   1988   917.55   88-600093
ISBN 0-943475-00-7 (pbk.)

Printed in the United States of America
U.S. Government Printing Office

☆ U.S. Government Printing Office: 1988 - 534-790

Contents

Foreword

America's natural and cultural history is revealed in her rural landscape. An awareness of the agricultural subsistence of rural America is becoming more elusive today, as historic buildings, old homesites, and barns crumble with age and misuse. Vegetation overtakes the remnants of our cultural heritage, and economic pressures convert greater amounts of green space and landscape into developments. Fortunately, efforts have been made to preserve and conserve the natural and cultural settings of early rural America through the protection and management of the rural landscape. The crest of the Blue Ridge Parkway was selected almost fifty years ago as the route of the first rural parkway in the world. Its purpose was to link Shenandoah National Park in Virginia and the Great Smoky Mountains National Park in North Carolina and Tennessee by way of a recreation-oriented motor road. Threading its way along much of the crest of the Appalachian Mountain chain for almost five hundred miles, the parkway provides a variety of opportunities for the motoring public. The parkway takes travelers quietly and leisurely through a living laboratory of mountain landscapes, plant and animal communities, and human lifestyles.

In locating and constructing the parkway, the objective was simple: to please the traveler by revealing the charm and interest of the countryside. This objective attempted to take advantage of land features such as fields, fences, streams, rock formations, woodlands, and wildflowers, as well as the distant mountain vistas.

Our role today is to protect and preserve the integrity of these natural features as well as the cultural and natural visual resources that make the parkway so unique. We want future generations to experience the independence, the self-sufficiency, and the pride of the mountain folk. At the same time, we want them to learn more about us, the National Park Service, and our stewardship responsibility.

This book is important because it offers guidance on the best possible use of our funds and manpower to protect and preserve our rural landscape. As we manage this important national treasure according to the mandate handed down by Congress, we want to ensure that the people's values are a key part of the decisions we make for the perpetuation of the visual resources along the Blue Ridge Parkway.

The research techniques and theories described in this book offer a useful guide to the management and protection of America's rural landscapes. In so doing, it provides a unique opportunity to better understand America's visual experience.

Gary Everhardt, Superintendent
Blue Ridge Parkway

Preface

Man's use of the natural environment frequently results in conflicting demands regarding the value of certain resources. Unlike Lester Ward's "telic" view of mankind, which described life as a struggle to gain control over natural resources (*Dynamic Sociology* 1883), much of man's effort today is directed at resolving conflicts between competing claims over how to use the natural environment. Solutions for resolving or reducing these competing demands usually involve some compromise. Aesthetic beauty—or the enjoyment of viewing scenic vistas of the natural landscape—reflects only one of the many competing uses society demands of its natural environment.

The Blue Ridge Parkway offers transportation, recreation, and culture to travelers who tour its 470-mile corridor through the crest of the southern Appalachians. However, the main feature of the parkway is the appeal of its scenic beauty. The parkway's travel brochures describe "past vistas of quiet natural beauty and rural landscapes lightly shaped by the activities of man. You travel the Southern Highlands, a land of forested mountains, exquisite during the flowering spring, cool in the green summer, colorful in the red autumn." How does man "lightly shape" nature to provide visual scenes that offer an enjoyable sightseeing experience? The research described in this book seeks to answer this question by focusing on the tourist as sightseer.

Our approach for this research was to unite different scientific disciplines through a single set of surveys to determine the travelers' preferences for scenic overlooks and scenes along the Blue Ridge Parkway. A cooperative effort was mounted to cut across disciplinary lines to obtain the visual preferences of travelers through the perspectives of the psychologist, sociologist, forest recreationist and landscape architect. All of these disciplines share an interest in trying to understand and predict what influences a traveler's sightseeing preferences, but no such common research effort had been attempted until this project.

No discipline by itself has all the answers, but this collective multidisciplinary effort provides a mosaic of the travelers' visual responses to the parkway. Scientists from each of the different disciplines decided what data was needed from the travelers, and together they acted in designing, planning, sampling, and obtaining that information from parkway travelers. Through this cooperation, much multidisciplinary information can be applied toward better maintenance practices, land use covenants, and plans for future parkway programs to increase the public's enjoyment of the Appalachian region.

The general reader should be forewarned regarding the language and technical terms used in this book. A working knowledge of statistics is assumed, and some language used by the researchers includes specialized technical terms that also require the reader to have some working knowledge of the disciplines. While we have attempted to mitigate these problems, we cannot totally eliminate them because of the advanced level of research that is being reported. Consequently, this book is written for the educated public, including advanced college students, academic and agency professionals, upper level management, and educated park tourists. These readers are likely to be the opinion leaders who will stimulate change in managing our park vistas.

The first chapter provides an overview explaining the kinds of information sought to aid resource managers in maintaining the vistas and vegetation along the parkway, and why. Chapter 2 reports how the parkway traveler ranks his preferences for certain parkway scenes. Chapter 3 further describes how parkway travelers rank these scenes, according to their socio-economic backgrounds. Chapter 4 attempts to explain the travelers' scenic preferences by evaluating their attitudes toward recreation and the environment. Chapter 5 shifts the emphasis toward the human visual nervous system and how it responds to scenes along the parkway, especially background and damaged vegetation. Chapter 6 tests the influence of communicative messages on an individual's scenic preferences. Chapters 7 and 8 are prepared by landscape architects who simulated parts of scenes along the parkway to measure how changes in vegetative management may affect preferences. The final chapter summarizes the researchers' basic findings and recommends management options toward ensuring continued visual enjoyment of the Blue Ridge Parkway.

The individual contributors wish to acknowledge with gratitude the review comments of the National Park Service Natural Resources Publications Review Board. In particular, we are grateful for the editorial contributions of Jim Wood, Science Publications Editor, National Park Service Scientific Monograph Series. Superintendent Gary Everhardt and his staff at the Blue Ridge Parkway have greatly facilitated and supported this multidisciplinary research effort.

Francis P. Noe   July 1987
Atlanta, Georgia

Contributors

Robert H. Becker is Professor with the Department of Parks, Recreation, and Tourism Management at Clemson University, Clemson, South Carolina. His major interests involve the human use of natural resources and the allocation of those resources among user groups.

Gregory J. Buhyoff is Professor of Forestry and Assistant Director for Research and Graduate Studies in the School of Forestry and Wildlife Resources at Virginia Polytechnic Institute and State University, Blacksburg, Virginia. His current interests are in quantitative applications in natural resource management.

Timothy R. Day is an Assistant Professor of Landscape Architecture at California State Polytechnic College, Pomona, California. His research interests include viewer resource management and computer applications in the fields of education, landscape architecture and planning.

F. Dominic Dottavio is currently Deputy Associate Regional Director for Science and Natural Resources in the Southeast Regional Office, National Park Service, Atlanta, Georgia. His interests are directed toward interdisciplinary work in both the social and natural sciences.

Nick R. Feimer is a Research Supervisor in Marketing with the Quaker Oaks Company, Chicago, Illinois.

William E. Hammitt is Professor of Forest Recreation in the Department of Forestry, Wildlife, and Fisheries at the University of Tennessee, Knoxville, Tennessee. His current interests involve visual perceptions of outdoor recreation environments and recreation behavior studies.

Gary D. Hampe is an Associate Professor of Sociology at the University of Wyoming, Laramie, Wyoming. His research interests are directed toward problems of aesthetic appreciation and park management. He also specializes in family and aging issues.

Barbara L. McDonald is a Research Coordinator with the Institute of Community and Area Development at the University of Georgia, Athens, Georgia. Her current interests concern the assessment of spiritual values of recreational experiences.

Francis P. Noe is a Research Sociologist with the National Park Service, Southeast Regional Office, Atlanta, Georgia and adjunct professor at a number of Southeast universities. His research focuses on national, regional, and park-specific issues and appears in sociological, environmental, and leisure-recreational journals.

James F. Palmer is a Senior Research Associate with the Faculty of Environmental Studies and Institute of Environmental Policy and Planning at the State University of New York, Syracuse, New York. He has published a number of articles and book chapters on environmental perception research and has received numerous research grants for studies addressing landscape perceptions and environmental attitudes.

Michael R. Patsfall is Senior Human Resource Representative with the Lockheed Space Operations Company at Kennedy Space Center, Titusville, Florida.

Tad Redway, III is a Project Manager with Environmental Planning and Design Associates, Portland, Maine. He previously worked as a graduate assistant on the Blue Ridge Study.

Lawrence Reichardt is a planner with the Monroe County Planning Department in Rochester, New York. He also worked as a graduate assistant with the Blue Ridge Study.

Richard C. Smardon is Director of the Institute for Environmental Policy and Planning at the State University of New York, Syracuse, New York. His research interests include visual resource management, wetland assessment and environmental management and administration.

J. Douglas Wellman is Associate Professor and Leader of the Wildland Recreation Section in the School of Forestry and Wildlife Resources at Virginia Polytechnic Institute and State University, Blacksburg, Virginia. His current interests are in wildland recreation policy and administration.

Chapter One
Introduction

Francis P. Noe
National Park Service
Southeast Regional Office
Atlanta, Georgia

William E. Hammitt
University of Tennessee
Knoxville, Tennessee

Background

Sightseeing is one of the most popular recreational activities in the United States. This fact is substantiated by many outdoor recreation preference studies conducted over the years. A recent survey by the Presidential Commission on Outdoor Recreation in America (New York Times, 1986) found that the most frequent outdoor activity is sightseeing. In various outdoor recreation research studies prepared by the Bureau of Outdoor Recreation (1968, 1973, 1977), sightseeing always appeared near the top of the list of user preferences. In Congress, the Interior and Insular Affairs Committee (September, 1974) predicted that by the year 2000, sightseeing would remain one of the nation's most popular outdoor recreation activities.

More site-specific surveys covering national parks throughout the United States report similar findings. A survey of visitors at Great Smoky Mountains National Park indicated that the more dilettantish tourist enjoys looking at pretty scenery and driving through pretty countryside without sacrificing his creature comforts. In almost every way, park visitors are more likely to be interested observers than active participants (ARMS Supplemental Report, Sept. 25, 1974). These findings were again confirmed in an updated review by Hammitt (1978) for the Great Smokies and nine other large national parks.

Despite the widespread evidence of the importance of sightseeing, we do not have an in-depth understanding about what constitutes a satisfying sightseeing experience—particularly as it relates to visual preference. Without knowing the visitors' most elementary sightseeing preferences, it is impossible for park managers to implement effective management and interpretive programs that will better enhance a park experience.

The sightseeing problem applies not only to the Blue Ridge Parkway but also has implications for other national parks, as the Park Service is charged with the preservation of the parks' natural resources and the protection of their aesthetic values. Almost no research has been conducted by government agencies or private scientists on this management problem. Since sightseeing remains one of the dominant activities of the American public, it is essential for us to learn as much as we can about its implications on the management of park resources.

In recent years, land use planners and managers in government agencies have become increasingly sensitive toward the public's demand for environmental attractiveness. Through the impetus of the National Environmental Policy Act of 1969 (Public Law 91–190), the federal government is required to act as the central participant in environmental quality to assure "safe, healthful, productive, and aesthetically and culturally pleasing surroundings." The Act further states in Section 102(b) that the government will ensure that presently unquantified environmental amenities and values may be given appropriate consideration in decision-making along with economic and technical considerations.

The legal consequences of the National Environmental Policy Act have resulted in a series of cases successfully challenged by plaintiffs on aesthetic grounds. A record of these court cases, compiled by Smardon (1984), shows that the courts are now willing to accept "enjoyment of scenic beauty as a legal right." Such legal action only heightens the need to acquire information about the scenic preferences of park tourists, so that covenants of use may be developed for park lands. More importantly, since national parks are often held up as scenic standards, public preferences need to be codified. For example, in *Scenic Hudson v. Federal Power Commission*, the plaintiff argued that the aesthetic "qualities" of the land being defended were equal to the landscapes in national parks and monuments. Such "park status" is interpreted as being beyond any claim for "power development and industrial purposes." However, since little quantitative empirical data exist on why national park lands are viewed as aesthetically pleasing, the management of these lands will be vulnerable to legal challenges until more is known about scenic preferences.

Gaining better perspectives on what tourists see as beautiful is also important to help park managers better understand "threats" to visual quality from inside and outside a park. In the recent State of the Parks Report to Congress (1980), the National Park Service listed 73 threats reported by resource managers that "have the potential to cause significant damage to park physical resources or to seriously degrade important park values or park visitor experiences." The single most significant category mentioned by park managers was aesthetic degradation, which accounted for 25% of the total number of reported threats. Aesthetic degradation was also one of the two highest areas of recognized threats that had the greatest need for adequate documentation. However, the factual basis for documenting these threats relied heavily on the perceptions of park managers, with no reliable input from park tourists. This disparity—between those charged with managing the resource and those enjoying the resource—needs to be resolved.

In the case of the Blue Ridge Parkway, there is a special urgency since the parkway staff has already anticipated that reductions in maintenance budgets could threaten the parkway's scenic vistas and so impact the tourists' visual experiences. According to the superintendent's staff (1981), "the Blue Ridge Parkway features scenic, recreational, and cultural resources of the Southern Appalachian Highlands. It is known throughout the world for its spectacular mountain and valley vistas, quiet pastoral scenes, sparkling streams and waterfalls, and colorful flower and foliage displays. The preservation of these scenic resources and the opportunity to see them depend upon the availability of parkway management to maintain the vista windows through which they are viewed. Hand labor is the only feasible method to accomplish vista clearing work. With the ever diminishing maintenance dollar and personnel ceilings, it is not possible to accomplish this work in a timely manner."

When the parkway was constructed during the 1930s, the original decisions regarding the provision and maintenance of scenic vistas were based largely on the professional judgments of the landscape architects of the time. Scientific methods of aesthetic research were then relatively new or simply did not exist. Today, however, the field of aesthetic research has now progressed to the point where user preferences of scenic vistas can be tested more empirically. Without hard evidence of the tourists' visual preferences of scenic vistas, little support for a position of labor-intensive maintenance can be justified. To help the parkway "scrutinize all vistas to make sure that those providing little benefit are dropped from the program" (Parkway Staff, 1981), tourist preferences are necessary to make accurate and reliable judgments. The question of determining what vistas to keep, drop, or modify is at the heart of this joint research effort.

The objectives of this study were to identify:

1. The types of vistas most and least preferred by the visitors of the Blue Ridge Parkway;
2. The levels and types of maintenance required to manage the preferred vistas;
3. The predictive basis for selecting new or eliminating present vistas; and
4. The relative importance of the visual experience along the different sections of the parkway.

Study Area

The Blue Ridge Parkway was established by Congress as a unit of the National Park System on June 30, 1936. Designed especially for motor recreation, the scenic drive extends about 470 miles through the southern Appalachian Mountains of western Virginia and North Carolina. The word "Appalachian" is reported to mean "subdued mountains." It aptly describes those mountains that were formed as a result of the process of erosion, which produced a covered mantle of deeply weathered rock, rounded peaks, and a blanketed forest cover (Fennemann 1938).

The Blue Ridge Parkway begins at Rockfish Gap, Virginia, adjacent to Shenandoah National Park, and ends at the eastern entrance of Great Smoky Mountains National Park near Cherokee, North Carolina (Fig. 1.1). The parkway traverses the crests and ridges of the Blue Ridge Province, which forms the core of the Appalachians; to the east is the Piedmont, and to the west is the Ridge and Valley Province.

Generally, the Piedmont Province is visible to the east and south, while the Ridge and Valley Province can be seen from various vantage points along the parkway's northern section. The combined physiography of these provinces provides the parkway tourist with a variety of scenic views.

Since the inception of the scenic parkway idea by Stanley Abbott in 1933 (Gignoux, 1986), the idea of a scenic route was paramount to the planners' and developers' objectives. Few topographic or detailed maps were available to offer much help. In the final analysis, "the procedure was for landscape architects and surveyors to traipse through the woods, talking with the local people about where the 'best views' were, working from one side of the ridge to the other, discussing the advantages, scenic and monetary, of locating the corridor here or there" (Blue Ridge Parkway, 1985). The parkway is nearing completion, but the process of identifying "best views" is an on-going process where maintenance of drive-offs, scenic overlooks, and vistas is concerned. The researchers contributing to this book on scenic preference, like the

Figure 1.1.   The Blue Ridge Parkway extends about 470 miles from Shenandoah National Park to Great Smoky Mountains National Park.

landscape architects of the 1930s, have surveyed the present-day users for their views, attitudes, and preferences. Since the Blue Ridge Parkway was designed to serve current users, their judgments gathered through modern survey techniques will serve as guidelines for management decisions.

Methods

Two basic studies were conducted. The first investigated visitor preferences for vista landscapes along the Blue Ridge Parkway. The second evaluated visitor preferences for vegetation management at selected overlooks and roadsides along the parkway. To introduce the reader to the overall project, the rest of this chapter will briefly summarize the research methods used for each of these two studies. The chapters that follow describe the specific methods peculiar to each of the researchers' disciplines. The sample questionnaires appear in Appendices A and B.

Vista Preference Study

Study Design. The Blue Ridge Parkway is a long linear park that traverses a variety of land forms, ranging from broad ridge and valley formations in the north to high elevation mountains in the south. To represent this degree of diversity, the parkway was divided into three geographical sections: the northern, middle, and southern.

The northern section extends about 116 miles south from the southern boundary of Shenandoah National Park to the Roanoke River, and is characterized by ridges and valleys. The middle section extends 210 miles from the Roanoke River to Bear Dam Overlook. This section is primarily a mountainous plateau and provides distant views of the Piedmont area. The southern section covers the remaining 144 miles to Great Smoky Mountains National Park and consists of mostly high elevation (5000 to 6000 ft) forested mountains.

Each section of the parkway was photographically inventoried, with the representative photographs of its overlook vistas designed into a photo-questionnaire. Thus, three photo-questionnaires were developed, corresponding to the variety of overlook vistas contained within each of the three geographical sections of the parkway.

Stimuli. Initially, all developed, pulloff, and overlook vistas along the parkway were photographed with a polaroid camera, catalogued, and grouped according to scenery and vegetative themes. From this inventory a set of vista scenes was selected to represent each of the scenery and vegetative themes identified. Three or more overlook scenes representing each theme were ultimately included in a photo-questionnaire.

Each overlook vista represented in the final photo-questionnaire was re-photographed using a 35-mm camera with a 50-millimeter lens. Photographs were taken from the most popular viewing point of each overlook, looking at the dominant view. The photos were in black and white and were taken in clear weather conditions.

Photo-questionnaire. The photo-questionnaires for the vista preference study consisted of four pages of photographs, followed by ten
pages of written questions. Although the photographs varied for each of
the three geographic sections of the parkway, the questions remained
constant in all three photo-questionnaires. The questions addressed the
visitors' current parkway trip plans and use patterns, past experiences
on the parkway, and various socioeconomic variables (Appendix A).

   The photo-questionnaires were printed in a booklet form with an attractive cover. The photographs, 32 for each section of the parkway,
were black and white, measured 2 × 3 in., and were printed eight to
the page. Printed directly below each photo was a 1–5 point Likert
scale for rating the visual preferences for the vista scenes (Nachmias,
1981). The preference rating scale consisted of the following categories:

   1 = dislike very much
   2 = dislike somewhat
   3 = neutral
   4 = like somewhat
   5 = like very much

Respondents indicated their degree of preference for each scene by simply circling the appropriate number below each photo.

Sample. Since summer tourists make up the majority of visitors to
the parkway, they were chosen as the sample population. Sampling was
conducted in August and September of 1982. Six pulloff overlooks
along the parkway were chosen for sampling visitors in each of the
three sections. The overlooks were selected based on high visitor use.
Visitors were asked to participate in the survey as they stopped their
vehicles to view the vistas. A record card containing names and ad-
dresses of the visitors, the identification number of the questionnaire,
and plans for their current parkway trip was completed for persons receiving a questionnaire. However, the respondents were asked to complete the questionnaire at their leisure and to mail it to us. One individual per vehicle was given a packet of materials containing a cover
letter explaining the purpose of the study, a copy of the questionnaire,
and a stamped, self-addressed envelope for returning the questionnaire.

   Photo-questionnaires were distributed to 300 visitors in each of the
three sections of the parkway. Sampling occurred on weekends and
weekdays as well as during most use-hours of the day. One week after
all questionnaires were distributed, a post card was sent to all respondents reminding them to return the survey. After two more weeks,
a second packet of materials—including another questionnaire, a return
envelope, and a cover letter—was sent to those individuals that had not
returned their first questionnaire. Two weeks following this, a final letter was sent urging individuals to respond if their questionnaire still

had not been returned. This follow-up procedure, as modified by Dillman et al. (1974), resulted in a return rate of 80% for all three sections of the parkway.

Vegetation Management Study

Study Design. The purpose of the vegetation management study was to obtain visitor reactions to various methods of vegetation management along the parkway. Three aspects of vegetation management were investigated: roadside grass mowing, trimming of foreground vegetation just beyond the road's edge, and cutting woody vegetation at vista overlooks. Photographs were used to represent these different techniques and levels of vegetation management. Some of the photographs were simulations, where the original photos were manipulated to represent various types of management by removing or adding vegetation.

Although we surveyed visitors in the three geographic sections of the parkway to get a representative sample, only one set of photographs was used. However, an additional version of the photo-questionnaire was developed. It included an information or message treatment page on the inside of the cover. The purpose of this treatment page was used to test the effects of a communicative message on the preferences and attitudes of participants toward vegetation management when all other factors were held constant.

Stimuli. Photographs of roadside mowing practices were obtained from a slide collection at Clemson University. Mowing alternatives ranged from no mowing, to mowing one mower width from the road's edge, to complete mowing from the edge of the road to the forest edge. Vista photos were obtained from the "vista preference study" just described. Thirty-six color photos were used, each measuring about 2 × 3 in.

Photo-questionnaire. The photo-questionnaire for the vegetation management study was printed in booklet form (Appendix B). Half of the questionnaires contained the message treatment page. The photos were printed six to the page, as three pairs of photos. The pairs of photos were matched sets in which one photo was a "control" or contained less vegetative manipulation than the other photo. The photo pairs were designed to allow a comparison of vegetation management practices. Below each photo was printed a preference scale of 1 through 5 and a brief statement. Each photo was rated using the 5-point Likert scale for how much one liked it as compared to its paired member. Following the photographs were four pages of questions that asked the respondents to give (1) their preferred vegetation management alternatives, (2) their outdoor recreation participation, (3) their leisure attitudes, and (4) their socioeconomic characteristics.

Sample. On-site sampling occurred during the last two weeks of August 1983. Popular vista pulloffs in each of the three sections of the parkway were used. Visitors were asked to participate in the study as they left their vehicles and approached the overlook areas. Six hundred visitors were surveyed, with every other person receiving a questionnaire containing the message treatment page.

As in the "vista preference study," each respondent was given a packet of materials (i.e., cover letter, photo-questionnaire, and stamped, self-addressed return envelope) and asked to complete it at his leisure. The same modified Dillman et al. (1974) system was used to encourage a good response rate. Respondents returned 504 usable questionnaires, an 84% response rate.

REFERENCES

Act of June 30, 1936. 49 Stat. 2041, as amended, establishing the Blue Ridge Parkway. 16 U.S.C. / 46 a-2, et seq.

Amusement/Recreation Marketing Service. 1974. *Supplemental Report on Visitor Sampling Survey: Great Smoky Mountains National Park*. New York: N.Y.

Blue Ridge Parkway. 1981. Threats to Parks Worksheet. Fiscal Year 1981 Plans. Parkway files, Asheville, N.C.

Blue Ridge Parkway. 1985. *50th Anniversary Blue Ridge Parkway*. Parkway files, Asheville, N.C.

Bureau of Outdoor Recreation. 1968. *The Recreational Imperative*. Washington, D.C.: U.S. Department of the Interior.

Bureau of Outdoor Recreation. 1973. *Outdoor Recreation: A Legacy For America*. Washington, D.C.: U.S.Department of the Interior.

Dillman, D., J. Christensen, R. Brooks and E. Carpenter. 1974. Increasing mail questionnaire response: a four state comparison. *American Sociological Review* 39: 755.

Fenneman, N.H. 1938. *Physiography of Eastern United States*. New York: McGraw-Hill Book Co.

Gignoux, Leslie. 1986. Stanley Abbott and the design of the Blue Ridge Parkway. In B.M. Buxton and S.M. Beatty (Eds.), *Blue Ridge Parkway*. Boone, NC: Appalachian Consortium Press.

Hammitt, William E. 1978. *Differences in Participation and Use Patterns at Some Major National Parks*. Contract A-4970. Washington, D.C.: Heritage Conservation and Recreation Service, U.S. Department of the Interior.

Heritage Conservation and Recreation Service. 1977. *The Third Nationwide Outdoor Recreation Plan*. Washington, D.C.: U.S. Department of the Interior.

Nachmias, N. 1981. *Research Methods in the Social Sciences*. New York: St. Martin's.

National Park Service. 1980. *State of the Parks—1980*. Washington, D.C.: U.S. Department of the Interior.

New York Times CXXXV (45), 1986. "Survey finds outdoor U.S. that wants nature areas kept."

Smardon, Richard. 1984. When is the pig in the parlor? The interface of legal and aesthetic considerations. *Environmental Review* 78(2):147–161.

U.S. Congress. 1974. Committee on Interior and Insular Affairs. Sept. *The Recreation Imperative*. Washington, D.C.: U.S.Government Printing Office.

Chapter Two
Visual and Management Preferences of Sightseers

William E. Hammitt
University of Tennessee
Knoxville, Tennessee

Driving for pleasure, sightseeing, and hiking are popular recreational pursuits that depend greatly on perceptions of the visual environment. Many of the benefits that recreationists receive from engaging in these and similar outdoor activities are directly related to how the visual environment is viewed, managed, and presented to the visitors (Hammitt, 1980; Mercer, 1975; Moeller et al., 1974).

In this chapter we analyze the perceptions of Blue Ridge Parkway visitors at vista scenes. The major purpose is to identify landscape themes or prototypes that visitors prefer to view. From this analysis a *visual preference typology* is developed for vistas of the parkway. A second purpose of the chapter is to discuss parkway visitor feelings toward vegetation management alternatives at parkway vistas and roadsides. The levels and types of vegetation management and their alternatives are examined.

Conceptual Approach

While viewing a scene, people are both looking at and assessing, though subconsciously, its visual content (Appleton, 1975; Arnheim, 1969; S. Kaplan, 1973). Not only do people analyze the content of natural landscapes, but they also have preferences concerning the visual content and information contained within the scenes. That is, visual preference for certain environments or landscapes depends largely on the visual resources perceived in that environment and the associated information being processed (Hammitt, 1983).

Developing the concept further, it is believed that the visitors' visual preferences for landscape scenes can be analyzed for the preferred visual content of the landscapes. Recent contributions in the area of measuring environmental perception and visual preference (Arthur and Boster, 1976) allow for the examination of visual resources and their management. Landscape elements (Shafer et al., 1969; Zube, 1976; Daniel and Boster, 1976; Arthur, 1977; Buhyoff and Wellman, 1980) and themes and content constructs (Wohlwill, 1968; R. Kaplan, 1973, 1975; S. Kaplan, 1979; Wohlwill and Harris, 1980; Hammitt, 1980) can be determined. This chapter focuses on identifying landscape themes that are visually preferred.

Also basic to the conceptual framework of this analysis is the belief that people are primarily "visual" processors of environmental information. The perception of natural environments is a complex process, involving all of our senses, our past experiences, and images in memory. However, it is vision that people depend on most for relating to the environment, particularly sightseeing environments like the Blue Ridge Parkway. Sight is of crucial importance and probably influences human response to environments more directly and with greater salience than the other senses (Welsh, 1966; Arnheim, 1969; Campbell, 1974). Even when the other senses are involved in processing environmental information, they are usually associated with a visual image, either called up from memory or existing in the physical environment.

Based on the theories that humans are primarily visual processors of environmental information, that the visual content of landscape themes is a primary determinant of visual preference for vistas, and that the visual content of vista landscapes can be altered through vegetation management practices, a visual preference survey was selected as an appropriate approach for studying the perceptions of Blue Ridge Parkway tourists. In addition, since the perceptions of major interest concerned pull-off vista scenes, photographs were determined to be a logical means for abstracting what tourists prefer during their visits to the parkway. Ratings of photographs have been determined through other studies to be equivalent to on-site perceptions, and an acceptable medium for evaluating visual preferences for landscapes (Boster and Daniel, 1972; Shafer and Richards, 1974).

Preference Analysis Procedures

Vista Preferences

Visual preference ratings (1 through 5) of individual photographs were averaged to compute a mean preference rating for each landscape scene. The mean rating values were used to rank the scenes from most to least preferred. Then, to identify underlying landscape themes, the photos' ratings were factor analyzed. The factor analysis procedure was simply a computerized means of reducing the large data set of photos to small groups of scenes that demonstrated a shared commonality in content. Principal Factoring with Interaction and Orthogonal Varimax Rotation from SPSS (Nie et al., 1975) was used for the factoring. Standard criteria used in selecting factors (groupings of similar vista scenes) were: factor loadings had to be >0.40 for a photo to be included in a factor; only factors with eigenvalues >1.0 were extracted; and the reliability coefficient (Cronbach's alpha) of factors had to be near 0.60 or greater for them to be retained (Nunnally, 1967). Once factors were determined, a factor mean was determined for each grouping of scenes. The factor means were used as a basis for interpreting the visual preferences of parkway visitors for the major vista landscapes and for determining a visual preference typology of parkway vistas.

Vegetation Management Preferences

Visual preference ratings (1 through 5) were obtained for similar pairs of photographs of vista and roadside scenes that illustrated different levels and types of vegetation management. Mean ratings of pairs of scenes in the comparison sets were tested, using T-tests, for differences in preference for the vegetation management alternatives. Visitor support for the various vegetation maintenance alternatives was also investigated. A six-point Likert type rating scale was used for recording level of support for the maintenance alternatives.

Preference for Vista Overlooks

Most and Least Preferred Scenes

Although it is impossible here to consider the preference ratings of all 96 photos surveyed, it is possible to report the ratings of the most and least preferred scenes for each of the three geographic sections of the parkway.

Mean preference ratings for the vista overlooks indicate visitors do have a range of preference for the various vistas along the parkway. The range of lowest and highest ratings, the range differential, and the overall mean rating for each section are reported in Table 2.1. The values indicate a general range in preference from a low of about 2.70 to a high of about 4.50. Thus, the preference values are skewed toward the upper end of the scale, indicating visitors liked the least preferred vistas "somewhat" and the most preferred vistas "quite a bit" to "very much." However, we found less difference in preference ratings for the three parkway sections than expected. It was anticipated that the higher peaks and the more remote mountainous scenery of the southern section

Table 2.1. Mean range of visual preference ratings for vista scenes in the southern, middle, and northern sections of the Blue Ridge Parkway.[1]

| Section | Range | | Range | Mean |
	Lowest – Highest		Differential	Difference
Southern	2.82	– 4.30	1.48	3.55
Middle	2.55	– 4.47	1.92	3.54
Northern	2.84	– 4.73	1.89	3.56

[1] Range and other values based on a 1 through 5 preference rating scale, where: 1 = liked not at all, 2 = a little, 3 = somewhat, 4 = quite a bit, 5 = liked very much.

would be more preferred than vistas of the middle and northern sections. This was not the situation, as vistas in the southern section received ratings equal to or even lower than the other two sections.

A comparative examination of the most and least preferred scenes reveals an obvious difference in vista landscape preference (Figure 2.1). Vista scenes most preferred along the parkway are those that include a water landscape. Fast-moving water scenes in the northern section received the highest ratings, while slow-moving river or pond scenes in the middle section were the most liked vista landscapes. Only one water landscape, a river scene, was included in the southern section photo set, but it was rated as the most preferred vista in that section. Vistas of water landscapes were consistently preferred by visitors, with the five water landscape photos in the northern section being rated as the top five preferred vistas. At the other extreme, the least preferred vistas were those in which the foreground and middleground woody vegetation has grown up to partially block the view of visitors. Again, this pattern was consistent across all three of the parkway sections.

Identifying Landscape Dimensions

To reduce the data set of 96 scenes to a manageable unit, the scenes were factor-analyzed into common landscape themes by parkway section. Based on the preference ratings for the vista scenes, the factor analysis procedure groups similarly rated photos and assists in the identification of landscape patterns or themes. It is much more practical to search for underlying patterns among the vista landscapes, for only in limited situations can one design or manage a landscape on an individual scene basis.

The factor analysis resulted in four landscape dimensions in each of the parkway sections. Each dimension was assigned a name, based on the general theme that characterized it. Because it is impractical to in-

SOUTHERN

$\overline{X}$ = 4.30 $\overline{X}$ = 2.82

MIDDLE

$\overline{X}$ = 4.45 $\overline{X}$ = 2.55

NORTHERN

$\overline{X}$ = 4.73 $\overline{X}$ = 2.84

Figure 2.1.   The most and least preferred vista scenes in the southern, middle, and northern sections of the Blue Ridge Parkway. The mean preference rating of each photo is included directly below it, where 1 = liked not at all and 5 = liked very much.

clude all the photos comprising each dimension, a brief description of the vista themes will be given, as well as one exemplary scene for each dimension. The reader, if he desires, could reconstruct the dimensions from the data presented in Tables 2.2, 2.4, and 2.6. Results of the analysis and descriptions of the themes are presented by geographic section of the parkway.

Southern Section

For the southern section, 21 of the 32 photos factored into the four dimensions identified (Table 2.2). Three of the dimensions had coherent scenes that were tightly grouped, with reliability values of 0.87 or higher. The fourth dimension, which contained scenes of developments in mountain valleys, was far less reliable (0.59). The four dimensions or vista themes were labeled, in order of visitor preference, as Several-

Table 2.2. Factor Analysis Results for southern section vistas (N = 197).

Vista Dimension And Photo No.	Factor Loading	Photo Mean	Factor Mean	Factor Alpha Value
SEVERAL-RIDGED				
3	0.7161	4.02		
23	0.7123	4.11		
31	0.6994	4.21		
2	0.6906	4.16	3.96	0.88
32	0.6005	3.71		
12	0.5899	3.84		
28	0.5604	3.68		
VALLEY DEVELOPMENT				
14	0.6562	3.50		
4	0.5291	4.05	3.57	0.59
22	0.4737	3.15		
UNMAINTAINED				
13	0.7264	3.54		
29	0.7251	3.19		
16	0.6769	2.84		
21	0.6580	3.18	3.36	0.89
18	0.6228	3.81		
9	0.5915	3.45		
24	0.5264	3.52		
ONE-RIDGED				
8	0.7690	2.83		
19	0.6817	3.26		
11	0.6488	3.23	3.19	0.88
15	0.5750	3.45		

Ridged Vista; Valley Development Vista; Unmaintained Vista; and One-Ridged Vista. Figure 2.2 contains a representative scene from each dimension.

Several-Ridged Vista. The seven photographs in this dimension are characterized by an open view of a series of mountainous ridges, usually three or more in depth. The vista landscapes contain a panoramic view with considerable depth of field. The series of mountainous peaks and valleys provide a number of mini-landscapes for the visitor to visually explore. All the scenes were heavily forested, with no evidence of human development. Other than the one water scene (Figure 2.1), which visitors rated high, the several-ridged mountain scenes were consistently among the most preferred vistas in the southern section (see photo means in Table 2.2).

A. Several-Ridged Vista   B. Valley Development Vista

C. Unmaintained Vista   D. One-Ridged Vista

Figure 2.2.   Example of one characteristic scene from each of the four dimensions of southern section vistas, Blue Ridge Parkway.

Valley Development Vista. Characteristic of this dimension were scenes of mountainous valleys that contained farm or rural community development (Figure 2.2, photo B). Two of the scenes were of distant developments, while the third was of a farm homestead in the middleground of the scene. Visitors varied in their preference for the developed scenes, as this dimension was not very reliable.

Unmaintained Vista. Scenes in this dimension are characterized by a view of one to two background mountain ridges in which the vista is partially blocked by foreground trees and shrubs. In most of the seven scenes, the foreground trees have grown up to block the view as the vista vegetation has matured, or the shrubs had not been cleared immediately adjacent to the pull-off vista. It appears visitors do not mind some vegetation in the foreground as long as the background view is not blocked. However, there is a definite trend toward lower preference as the foreground trees increase.

One-Ridged Vista. The least preferred vista landscape theme in the southern section involved scenes that included only one mountainous ridge (Figure 2.2, photo D). All four scenes in this grouping were very similar—open views of a rounded mountain ridge that occupied three-fourths of the vista. When compared to the scenes in the Several-Ridged Vista dimension, the One-Ridged Vista scenes offer far less opportunity for visual involvement.

Mean values for the four dimensions ranged from a high of 3.96 for the Several-Ridged Vista to a low of 3.19 for the One-Ridged Vista. When compared, the means proved to be significantly different (Table 2.3). In terms of practical significance, the dimensions also appear thematically different and help identify distinct aspects of the southern section for vista-management purposes.

Middle Section

Twenty-eight of the 32 photos of the middle section factored into the four dimensions identified (Table 2.4). However, two of the dimensions accounted for 22 of the scenes and 809 of the variance. All four of the dimensions had acceptable reliability coefficients, ranging from 0.90 to 0.69. The four landscape dimensions were named: Pond/Lake Vista, Rolling Plateau Vista, One-Ridged Vista, and Unmaintained Vista.

Pond/Lake Vista. This dimension contains four vistas that include a pond or lake waterscape surrounded by trees as the dominant view (Figure 2.3, photo A). Three of the scenes appear as pond or small lake waterscapes in the middleground, and all have mean preference ratings above 4.0. The one distant view of a reservoir scene received a lower

Table 2.3. Comparison of preference means for the four vista dimensions in the southern section.

Vista Dimension	Mean	t-value[1]	Significance
Several-Ridged	3.96	5.80	0.001
Valley Development	3.57	−3.86	0.001
Unmaintained	3.36	2.83	0.005
One-Ridged	3.19		

[1] Based on proximate pairs of dimensions.

Table 2.4. Factor analysis results for middle section vistas (N = 212).

Vista Dimension And Photo No.	Factor Loading	Photo Mean	Factor Mean	Factor Alpha Value
POND/LAKE				
6	0.6653	4.16		
11	0.6608	4.45		
32	0.6505	4.30	4.12	0.75
14	0.4732	3.57		
ROLLING PLATEAU				
27	0.8042	3.89		
22	0.7427	4.16		
17	0.7424	3.99		
25	0.7380	3.94		
23	0.7377	3.35		
4	0.6822	3.95		
1	0.6144	3.66	3.75	0.90
26	0.6227	3.90		
9	0.5940	4.12		
20	0.5357	3.12		
15	0.5185	3.62		
12	0.5181	3.46		
ONE-RIDGED				
31	0.6055	3.57	3.68	0.69
28	0.5727	3.80		
UNMAINTAINED				
8	0.7563	2.57		
13	0.6829	2.78		
3	0.6768	2.75		
2	0.6210	3.19		
19	0.5988	2.97		
7	0.5978	3.54	2.99	0.88
16	0.5521	2.76		
18	0.5391	3.21		
29	0.5357	3.19		
21	0.4710	2.96		

rating of 3.57. Also, based on the factor analysis values, the three pond scenes are much more characteristic of this dimension.

Rolling Plateau Vista. The 12 scenes making up this dimension are characterized by rolling, broad plateau valleys that include a mosaic of farm, pastureland, and hardwood forest (Figure 2.3, photo B). The amount of pasture and farmland in the scenes varied from approximately 60% to less than 10%. Those photos containing 50% or more pasture areas were rated high in preference, with mean ratings of 3.8 to 4.1. These landscapes offer more opportunity for visual involvement and readability, as fields and forests add greater coherence, legibility, textural diversity, and complexity to the scenes.

A. Pond/Lake Vista

B. Rolling Plateau Vista

C. One-Ridged Vista

D. Unmaintained Vista

Figure 2.3.   Example of one characteristic scene from each of the four dimensions of middle section vistas, Blue Ridge Parkway.

One-Ridged Vista. Scenes in this dimension are almost identical to those in the One-Ridged dimension of the southern section, being dominated by a single, rounded ridge with little variation in relief.

Unmaintained Vista. The least preferred of any vista dimensions ($\bar{X}$ = 2.99) in all three sections was the unmaintained vista, where tree vegetation has matured to the point that the view was partially blocked (Figure 2.3, photo D). In most of the scenes, one-half to three-fourths of the vista landscape was blocked from view. Foreground and middleground trees are a more serious problem in the middle section than the southern section, for the lower elevation and relief of the middle section allows the trees to block more of the vista. At several of the vistas, considerable clearing of vegetation in the foreground and middleground will be necessary to return the overlook vistas to their original condition or to a condition preferred by parkway visitors.

The mean preference values for the four dimensions in the middle section (Table 2.5) indicate a greater range in preference values than that for the southern section. The Pond/Lake scenes received a high of 4.12, while the Unmaintained dimension was rated 2.99. However, the Rolling Plateau ($\bar{X}$ = 3.75) and the One-Ridged ($\bar{X}$ = 3.68) Vistas were not rated significantly different. Both were liked fairly well.

Table 2.5. Comparison of preference means for the four vista dimensions in the middle section.

Vista Dimension	Mean	t-value[1]	Significance
Pond/Lake	4.12	−6.14	0.001
Rolling Plateau	3.75	0 76	0.448
One Ridged	3.68	−11.31	0.001
Unmaintained	2.99		

[1] Based on proximate pairs of dimensions.

Northern Section

All but four of the 3 northern section photos factored into the four vista dimensions identified (Table 2.6). One factor, dominated by scenes of the open ridged and valley landscape, contained 15 of the photos and accounted for 65% of the variance. The reliability coefficients of the four dimensions ranged from 0.94 to 0.68. Labels assigned to the dimension were: Stream/River Vista, Farm Valley Vista, Ridge and Valley Vista, and Unmaintained Vista.

Stream/River Vista. The four scenes comprising this vista type show rapidly moving water in forested settings (Figure 2.4, photo A). Two

Table 2.6. Factor analysis results for northern section vistas (N = 171).

Vista Dimension and Photo No.	Factor Loading	Photo Mean	Factor Mean	Factor Alpha Value
STREAM/RIVER				
18	0.6772	4.56		
4	0.6583	4.68		
10	0.5301	4.73	4.61	0.68
2	0.4402	4.47		
FARM VALLEY				
26	0.7243	3.64		
5	0.5348	3.70	3.60	0.75
29	0.4990	3.44		
RIDGE AND VALLEY				
3	0.8000	3.75		
21	0.7943	3.10		
14	0.7773	3.77		
19	0.7534	3.36		
9	0.7435	3.54		
15	0.7307	3.39		
11	0.7208	3.26		
13	0.7027	3.32	3.46	0.94
16	0.6939	3.39		
6	0.6854	3.30		
1	0.6596	3.44		
8	0.6585	3.09		
12	0.6051	3.75		
22	0.5562	3.69		
30	0.4982	3.81		
UNMAINTAINED				
23	0.7848	3.01		
20	0.7372	2.84		
25	0.7124	3.26		
28	0.7051	3.21	3.21	0.87
32	0.5966	3.53		
7	0.5716	3.39		

photos are of fast-moving streams or rivers having white water, one photo is a waterfall, and the other photo is a river in which the current is visible. These four scenes of rapidly moving water were the most highly preferred vistas among the 96 photos rated in the three parkway sections. The four individual photo preference means ranged from 4.73 to 4.47. The water scenes of this section seem to differ most from those of the middle section by having rapidly moving white water rather than still water, pond-like settings, and more forested surroundings.

Farm Valley Vista. Views of broad, open valleys in which farm fields dominate the scene are characteristic of this dimension (Figure 2.4, photo B). The scenes are somewhat similar to the pastoral scenes of the Rolling Plateau Vista in the middle section, except that the Farm Valley scenes are much more dominated by grassy fields and open valleys. Forests comprise less than 50% of each of the scenes. Visual preferences for the Farm Valley and the Rolling Plateau Vistas were similar, being 3.60 and 3.75, respectively.

Ridge and Valley Vista. Scenes of the Ridge and Valley Vista are characteristic of the ridge and valley physiography, consisting of low elevational, parallel ridges intersected with broad agricultural valleys (Figure 2.4, photo C). Two general groups of scenes are included in the

A. Stream/River Vista   B. Farm Valley Vista

C. Ridge And Valley Vista   D. Unmaintained Vista

Figure 2.4.   Example of one characteristic scene from each of the four dimensions of the northern section vistas, Blue Ridge Parkway.

dimension, one containing seven photos with valley development and another of eight photos where the broad valleys remain forested. Even in the valley-development scenes, the valleys appear in the middle to far background of the vistas and comprise usually less than 20% of the landscape in both groups of photos. The visual preference mean was 3.46.

Unmaintained Vista. As in the middle section, vistas that are becoming blocked by unmaintained vegetation are the least preferred by parkway visitors. The six photos in this dimension are essentially identical to those in the Unmaintained Vista of the middle section. However, the preference mean did not drop as low as it did in the middle section (3.21 vs. 2.99) primarily because of fewer scenes with immediate foreground vegetation blocking the view. Vistas with foreground tree and shrub vegetation that block the view are rated lower than vistas containing middleground vegetation.

The very high preference rating of the Stream/River Vista led to the widest range in vista dimension means being in the northern geographic section of the parkway (Table 2.7). The means ranged from a high of 4.61 for the rapidly moving water scenes to a low of 3.21 for the unmaintained scenes. All proximate pairs of the dimension means were significantly different at the 0.05 probability level.

Table 2.7. Comparison of preference means for the four vista dimensions in the northern section.

Vista Dimension	Mean	t-value[1]	Significance
Stream/River	4.61		
		− 16.03	0.001
Farm Valley	3 60		
		− 2.18	0.031
Ridge and Valley	3.46		
		4.18	0.001
Unmaintained	3.21		

[1] Based on proximate pairs of dimensions.

A Vista Preference Typology

When one examines the visual content of the landscape themes composing the 12 vista dimensions, some similarities and overlap are noted among the dimensions. Water, ridge and valley scenes with pastoral development, one-ridged mountain, and unmaintained vistas are common to two or more of the sections. Furthermore, when the 12 vista dimensions are ranked from high to low on the basis of visual preference, the dimensions naturally fall into larger groupings that have surprisingly common themes (Table 2.8).

Table 2.8. A visual preference of vista landscapes as pull-off overlooks along the Blue Ridge Parkway.

	Means	Vista Dimensions	Typology
HIGH PREFERENCE			
	4.61	Stream/River	⎤ WATER VISTAS
	4.12	Pond/Lake	⎦
	3.96	Several-Ridged	⎤ MULTI-RIDGED VISTAS
	3.75	Rolling Plateau	⎤
	3.68	One-Ridged	
	3.60	Farm Valley	PASTORAL VISTAS
	3.57	Valley Development	
	3.46	Ridge & Valley	⎦
	3.36	Unmaintained	⎤
	3.21	Unmaintained	UNMAINTAINED VISTAS
	3.19	One-Ridged	
	2.99	Unmaintained	⎦
LOW PREFERENCE			

Only the One-Ridged dimension does not follow the identified pattern. This pattern of commonality among the vista landscapes, based on preference ratings, provides a *Vista Preference Typology* for the Blue Ridge Parkway. Based on our data, visitors to the parkway prefer to see mountainous vistas of:

> Most Preferred
>> Rapidly Moving Water
>> Stationary Water
>> Mountains with Several Ridges
>> Pastoral Development
>> Mountains with One Ridge
>> Unmaintained Vegetation
>
> Least Preferred

This typology of vista preference can assist recreation planners and managers in the allocation of resources toward overlook development and maintenance. During the design stages of a scenic parkway project, the emphasis should be devoted to locating preferred vista landscapes. Water is a major attraction for many outdoor recreational activities, and sightseeing appears to be no exception. Perhaps of greater importance than the identification of preferred vistas is the finding that unmaintained vistas rank low in preference. The unmaintained vistas are a vegetation management problem, one that can be improved if open views are created at these overlooks. Various types and levels of vegetation management can be practiced at overlooks. The following section discusses the visitor preferences of some vegetation management alternatives on the Blue Ridge Parkway.

Vegetation Management Preferences

In addition to investigating vegetation management at overlook vistas, the visitors' preferences for different levels of roadside maintenance (i.e., grass mowing) were investigated. Comparative sets of photos that demonstrated a "control" scene and altered scenes with different levels of vegetation management were rated for preference. First, we will report visitor preferences concerning the clearing of woody vegetation at overlook vistas and then their preferences for grass mowing on parkway roadsides.

Vista Vegetation Comparisons

The mean preference ratings for the control and altered scenes of each comparative photo set are presented in Table 2.9. The photo pairs have been grouped according to patterns of visitor preference response, for interpretive purposes. Again, because of the impracticality of printing all photo sets, only characteristic examples are provided. However, a sample questionnaire of the 1983 survey is available in Appendix B, and the reader is referred to it for a more detailed interpretation.

The ratings in Table 2.9 indicate that the clearing of dense vegetation from the foreground of vistas generated the greatest difference (increase) in preference ratings. Photographs 16a and 10a contain vistas where 60 to 80% of the view is blocked (Figure 2.5, photos 10a and 10b). Removal of an appropriate amount, but not all, of the trees to re-open the vistas greatly increased visitor preference. The low preference for the unmaintained vistas agrees with the results from the vista overlook preference study just reported. The importance of foreground vegetation as a determinant of vista preference also agrees with the findings of Wellman et al. in Chapter 5.

The second grouping of photos in Table 2.9 consisted of five vista scenes in which the view was only partially blocked, approximately 20 to 50% (Figure 2.5, photos 12a and 12b). None of these scenes received a statistically significant increase in preference when the vegetation was cleared or partially cleared. However, four of the five photo pairs showed slight increases in preference for the treated photos. Visitors appear to be willing to tolerate a portion of the vista being blocked by vegetation.

The last three photo pairs in Table 2.9 indicate a higher preference mean for the control photos. In all three pairs, the control photos consisted of a scene where low foreground shrubs or trees block less than 20% of the view (Figure 2.5, photos 17a and 17b). Also, the treatments were selective in what vegetation was removed, and only a portion of

Table 2.9. Mean preference ratings for control and vegetation treatment photo pairs of vista scenes for the Blue Ridge Parkway.

PHOTO PAIR	PHOTO PAIR MEANS [1]		MEAN DIFFERENCE	SIGNIFICANCE
	Control	Treatment		
16a – 16b	1.95	4.51	2.55	0.001
10a – 10b	2.12	4.25	2.15	0.001
11a – 11b	3.37	3.68	0.31	0.054
18a – 18b	3.39	3.14	0.25	0.095
13a – 13b	2.89	3.12	0.25	0.184
12a – 12b	3.14	3.30	0.16	0.339
15a – 15b	2.86	3.02	0.16	0.303
14a – 14b	3.97	2.61	1.36	0.001
5a – 5b	3.65	2.46	1.19	0.001
17a – 17b	3.89	2.17	1.18	0.001

[1] Means are based on a visual preference rating scale, where 1 = liked not at all and 5 = liked very much.

the vegetation in two of the three photos was removed. Removal of hardwoods to emphasize conifers, the use of controlled burning to manage shrubs, or the complete removal of foreground shrubs was not a preferred management practice in these scenes where existing vegetation blocked little of the vista.

Although the number of vista photo pairs tested is limited, the data tend to indicate that vegetation management at unmaintained vistas where trees block a major portion of the view can greatly increase the visual preference for these scenes. However, visitors are willing to tolerate a certain degree of vegetation in a vista, as long as the view is less than 30 to 40% blocked. In fact, visitors tend to prefer some low foreground vegetation in a vista and may have little preference for selective management of hardwood vs. conifer species. However, further research is needed to verify these tentative findings.

Roadside Vegetation Comparisons

The preference ratings for the roadside mowing scenes are arranged into two groupings in Table 2.10: those scenes where the control photos were most preferred and those where the treatments were most preferred. As we will learn from inspecting the photos, they also fall into either group based on visual content or theme.

The first five photo pairs in Table 2.10 show a significantly higher preference for roadside scenes where the vegetation is mowed only one mower width (approximately 7 feet) from the pavement (Figure 2.6, photo 2a). Mowing beyond the guardrail or completely to the treeline

10a   10b

$\overline{X}$ = 2.12   Trees closing in the
scenic vista.

$\overline{X}$ = 4.25   Low shrubs in distant
foreground.

12a   12b

$\overline{X}$ = 3.14   Foreground trees in vista.

$\overline{X}$ = 3.30   No foreground trees in
vista.

17a   17b

$\overline{X}$ = 3.89   Low shrubs in distant
foreground.

$\overline{X}$ = 2.17   Mowing and cutting of
foreground vegetation.

Figure 2.5.   Example of characteristic photograph pairs from Table 2.9, illustrating different levels of vegetation treatment at Blue Ridge Parkway pull-off vistas. Photos "a" are the controls, "b" the treatments.

Table 2.10. Mean preference ratings for control and vegetation treatment photo pairs of roadside scenes, Blue Ridge Parkway.

PHOTO PAIR	PHOTO PAIR MEANS[1]			MEAN DIFFERENCE	SIGNIFICANCE
	Control		Treatment		
1a – 1b	4.02	<—	2.30	1.72	0.001
7b – 7a[2]	3.87	<—	2.68	1.19	0.001
2a – 2b	3.75	<—	2.79	0.95	0.001
9a – 9b	3.45	<—	2.81	0.64	0.001
6a – 6b	3.57	<—	3.09	0.47	0.007
4a – 4b	1.87	—>	4.23	2.36	0.001
8a – 8b	2.87	—>	3.32	0.45	0.003
3a – 3b	2.73	—>	3.02	0.29	0.094

[1] Means are based on a visual preference rating scale, where 1 = liked not at all and 5 = liked very much.
[2] The positions of the control and treatment photos were reversed in the questionnaire.

was less preferred in all these photos (see photo pairs, 1983 survey in Appendix B). A confounding variable in the control scenes is the presence of summer wildflowers, which no doubt increased preference for the control scenes. However, to encourage summer wildflowers along the roadside is to prohibit widescale mowing on a regularly scheduled basis.

The last three photo sets in Table 2.10 consist of scenes that appear more manipulated, or less natural, than the first five scenes. Only grasses were present in the photos. The roadside interpretive sign and the grassy, lawn-type situation (Figure 2.6, photos 4 and 8) were more preferred if managed more intensively. However, even mowing completely to the treeline in these situations may not be a preferred practice (photo 3, Appendix B). As with the vistas, visitors may have a threshold beyond which too much or too little vegetation management is an unpreferred state, and the threshold may be specifically related to the form of vegetation present. Wohlwill and Harris (1980) found evidence for a similar situation concerning the "fittingness" of man-made features in natural recreation settings. A man-made feature (i.e., interpretive sign) may be more in harmony with the environmental setting if the surrounding vegetation is managed more intensely than normal.

It is acknowledged that other studies (Anderson, 1981; Hodgson and Thayer, 1980) have shown that "labels" associated with photos (i.e., reservoir vs. natural lake) can influence preference ratings for visual scenes. The captions under our photo pairs may have had a similar

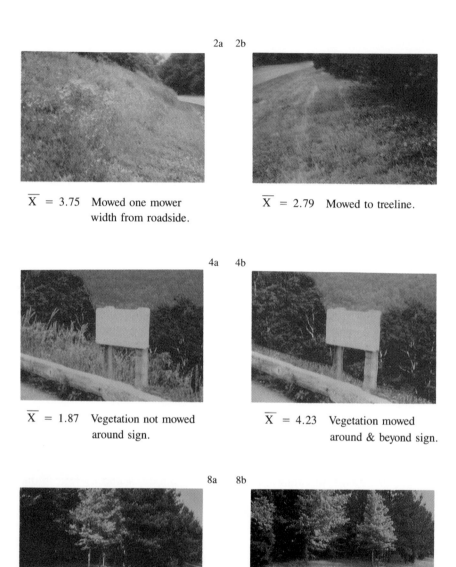

2a   2b

$\overline{X}$ = 3.75   Mowed one mower width from roadside.

$\overline{X}$ = 2.79   Mowed to treeline.

4a   4b

$\overline{X}$ = 1.87   Vegetation not mowed around sign.

$\overline{X}$ = 4.23   Vegetation mowed around & beyond sign.

8a   8b

$\overline{X}$ = 2.87   Mowed only at mid-summer.

$\overline{X}$ = 3.32   Mowed every three weeks.

Figure 2.6.   Example of characteristic photograph pairs from Table 2.10, illustrating different levels of vegetation treatment at Blue Ridge Parkway roadsides. Photos "a" are the controls, "b" the treatments.

influence. However, our captions were different from the labels of previous studies in that they denoted levels of management rather than the bipolar nature of natural vs. manipulated. The intention of our captions was to cue visitors to the level of vegetation management practiced in each pair of photos. In several photo pairs, sensitive words, such as *mowed*, were used for both the control and treatment photos.

Vegetation Maintenance Alternatives

In addition to the photo preference ratings for the vegetation management practices, visitors were asked to indicate their level of support for various levels of vegetation maintenance at vistas and roadsides. Three statements described levels of vista maintenance, while nine items were devoted to roadside vegetation maintenance. The items were developed to complement the management alternatives included in the photo comparisons and captions just discussed (Table 2.11); however, the statements were not associated with photographs.

A six-point Likert rating scale, where 1 = strongly support and 6 = definitely don't support, was used to record the visitors' level of support. For presentation here the six-point support scale was condensed to a three-level scale. "Strongly support" and "support" were combined, forming "support." "Probably support" and "probably don't support" formed an "indefinite" category. "Don't support" and "definitely don't support" were combined into a "non-support" category. The percentage of visitor support by these three categories is reported in Table 2.11.

Little difference occurs in terms of "support" among the three maintenance options for vistas. Approximately 40% of the visitors support the options of: annual clearing of vegetation, clearing every five to seven years, or clearing just often enough to maintain two-thirds of the view open (Table 2.11). Closer observation of the six original response levels indicates that 25% did "strongly support" annual cutting to maintain a completely open view. There was some difference in the "non-support" category, with fewer (14%) of the visitors not supporting the option of clearing foreground vegetation on a five to seven year basis. Overall, there seems to be no definite preference for any particular vista option. This may be because none of the practices involves the clearing of a vista that is more than one-third blocked by vegetation. In the vista photo-pairs, more than one-third of the vista had to be blocked before visitors reacted in a significant way.

In terms of maintenance options for roadsides, the grass-mowing practices supported most were: only one mower width from roadside (46%) and mowing only when necessary to maintain driver safety and help prevent grass fires (37%). However, the latter option had an equal

Table 2.11. Level of visitor support for vegetation maintenance alternatives at pull-off vistas and roadsides, Blue Ridge Parkway.

MAINTENANCE OPTION	LEVEL OF SUPPORT (%)			Don't Know
	Support	Indefinite	Non-support	
Shrubs and trees at pull-off vistas should be cut or trimmed:				
annually to maintain a completely clear view	41	25	28	6
every 5 to 7 years, before the shrubs in the foreground block much of the distant view	42	35	14	9
just often enough so that no more than ⅓ of the view is blocked	40	31	23	6
The roadside grass should be mowed:				
weekly, like a lawn	7	15	74	4
every two weeks, when 3 to 6 inches tall	31	28	36	5
once per month, when at least 10 inches tall	32	34	27	7
once in the Fall after the wildflowers are through blooming	41	23	27	9
only one mower width (7 ft) from the edge of the road surface	46	28	21	5
two mower widths (14 ft) from the road's edge	19	38	33	10
from the road's edge to the ditch or swale	24	39	20	17
from the road's edge to the treeline	23	26	44	7
as little as possible, only when necessary to maintain driver safety and help prevent grass fires	37	23	36	4

number of people who did not support the practice. Those practices least supported were mowing weekly (74%) and mowing from the road's edge to the treeline (44%). Nearly three-quarters of the respondents said they "definitely don't support" the weekly mowing of roadsides, and nearly one-half gave the same response for mowing to the treeline. Visitors were quite "indefinite" about mowing from the road's edge to the ditch or swale. This indecisiveness may be related to not knowing how far the ditch or swale may be from the roadside. Of the 39% that was "indefinite," nearly 25% said they probably supported the practice.

Support for the roadside maintenance options is in close agreement with the preference ratings of the roadside vegetation treatments in the photographic pairs. Mowing one mower width from the roadside, until the fall when wildflowers finish blooming, is the preferred maintenance option of the majority of our respondents. Mowing on a frequent basis and mowing all the way to the treeline were not supported by the visitors.

Summary and Implications

Although the entire Blue Ridge Parkway is a heavily used scenic resource, it does contain certain elements that are more preferred than others by the visiting public. The Blue Ridge Parkway, like any visual landscape, is also a dynamic resource, changing over time with the growth and successional development of native vegetation. As a result, the scenic overlooks and roadsides of the parkway must be monitored and managed continually to maintain the scenic benefits so desired by the public. The purposes of our study were to do exactly these: to assess visitor preferences for parkway pull-off vistas and to evaluate options for managing the vegetation at vistas and roadsides along the parkway.

In surveying visitor preferences for the many vista landscapes along the parkway, it was speculated that visitors would prefer the natural and mountainous scenes in the southern portion of the parkway over those in the more rolling physiographic sections to the north. For this reason three sub-surveys were conducted, based on vistas from each of the three sections of the parkway: southern, middle, and northern. This expectation did not materialize, as the range of preference ratings for the middle and northern sections was just as high as that in the southern section.

The mean preference ratings indicate that vistas containing waterscapes were the most preferred. Unmaintained vistas, with foreground and middle ground vegetation blocking 50% or more of the view, were least preferred. Mean preference for landscape vista themes, as determined by factor analysis, suggests a *Vista Preference Typology* for the parkway. The typology, based on those vista landscape themes most to least preferred, is as follows:

Most Preferred

> Rapidly Moving Water (Streams Rivers)
> Stationary Water (Ponds & Lakes)
> Mountains with Several Ridges
> Pastoral Development
> Mountains with One Ridge
> Unmaintained Vegetation

Least Preferred

This Vista Preference Typology can serve as a basis for the design and development of pull-off vistas, as well as for the allocation of resources toward the management and maintenance of vistas. Water has long been known to be a major attribute of many outdoor recreational activities, and sightseeing appears to be no exception. Perhaps of greater importance is the finding that the unmaintained vistas rank lowest in preference. The unmaintained vistas represent a vegetation management problem that can be improved if budgetary resources are made available to open up the views at these overlooks.

When asked to indicate their preference for various types and levels of vegetation management at vistas and along roadsides, visitors showed some definite preferences. Although our data is by no means conclusive, it does imply that:

1. People can differentiate between different types and levels of vegetation management. They have some definite preferences and non-preferences concerning vegetation maintenance practices along a scenic parkway.
2. Re-opening of vistas where vegetation blocks over 50% of the view can greatly enhance visual preference for these scenes. However, the public is willing to tolerate vegetation blocking a small portion of the view, and may even prefer a small amount of low foreground vegetation.
3. Roadside scenes that contain less grass mowing and more summer wildflowers are highly preferred. Roadside scenes that are more developed (i.e., interpretive signs) are more preferred if the grass is regularly mowed.
4. Roadside maintenance practices most preferred by visitors include the mowing of one mower width from the road's edge and only mowing in the fall after wildflowers have bloomed. Conversely, visitors least support the options of mowing on a frequent basis and all the way to the forest edge.

In conclusion, the vista and vegetation management preferences expressed by our sample of Blue Ridge Parkway visitors suggest that the public can be an important component in the management of scenic resources. These scenic resources are an important element in the leisure experience of parkway visitors, for the parkway is primarily a visual resource and its users are sightseers of landscapes. It is imperative that we include their input in the management of the parkway.

REFERENCES

Anderson, L.M. 1981. Land use designations effect perception of scenic beauty in forest landscapes. *Forest Science* 27 (2): 392–400.

Appleton, J. 1975. *The Experience of Landscapes*. New York: John Wiley and Sons.

Arnheim, R. 1969. *Visual Thinking*. Berkeley: University of California Press.

Arthur, L.M. 1977. Predicting scenic beauty of forest environments: Some empirical tests. *Forest Science* 23(2): 151–160.

Arthur, L. M., and R. S. Boster. 1976. Measuring scenic beauty: A selected annotated bibliography. USDA Forest Service General Technical Report RM-25, 34 p. Rocky Mtn. Forest and Range Exp. Stn., Ft. Collins, CO.

Boster, R.S., and T. C. Daniel. 1972. Measuring public response to vegetative management. p. 38–43. In Proc. 16th Annual Arizona Watershed Symposium, Arizona Water Comm., Phoenix.

Buhyoff, G.J., and J. D. Wellman. 1980. The specification of a nonlinear psychophysical function for visual landscape dimensions. *Journal of Leisure Research* 12(3): 257–272.

Campbell, B.G. 1974. *Human Evolution An Introduction to Man's Adaption*. Chicago: Aldine Publishing Co.

Daniel, T.C., and R. S. Boster. 1976. Measuring landscape esthetics: The scenic beauty estimation method. USDA Forest Service Research Paper RM-167, 66 p. Rocky Mtn. Forest and Range Exp. Stn., Ft. Collins, CO.

Hammitt, W.E. 1980. Managing bog environments for recreational experiences. *Environmental Management* 4(5): 425–431.

Hammitt, W.E. 1983. Assessing visual preference and familiarity for a bog environment. Chapter 6, *In* R. Smardon (Ed.). *The Future of Wetlands: Assessing Visual-Cultural Values*. Totowa, N.J.: Allanheld, Osmun Publishers.

Hodgson, R.W., and R. L. Thayer, Jr. 1980. Implied human influence reduces landscape beauty. *Landscape Planning* 7(2): 171–179.

Kaplan, R. 1973. Some methods and strategies in the predictions of preference. *In* E.H. Zube, R.O. Brush, and J.G. Fabos (Eds.) *Landscape Assessment Values, Perceptions, and Resources.* Stroudsburg, PA.: Dowden, Hutchinson and Ross.

Kaplan, R. 1975. Predictors of environmental preference: Designers and clients. *In* W.F.E. Preiser (Ed.). *Environmental Design Research.* Stroudsburg, PA.: Dowden, Hutchinson and Ross.

Kaplan, S. 1973. Cognitive maps in perception and thought. *In* R.M. Downs and D. Steal (Eds.). *Image and Environment.* Chicago: Aldine Press.

Kaplan, S. 1979. Concerning the power of content-identifying methodologies. In T. Daniel, E. Zube, and B. Driver (tech. coord.). *Assessing Amenity Resource Values.* USDA Forest Service General Technical Report RM-68, 70 p. Rocky Mtn. Forest and Range Exp. Stn., Ft. Collins, CO.

Mercer, D. 1975. Perception in outdoor recreation. In Patrick Lavery (Ed.) *Recreation Geography.* New York: Halstead Press.

Moeller, G.H., R. MacLachlan, and D. A. Morrison. 1974. Measuring perception of elements in outdoor environments. USDA Forest Service Research Paper NE-289, 9 p. Northeastern Forest Exp. Stn., Upper Darby, PA.

Nie, N.H., C. H. Hull, J. C. Jenkins, K. Steinbrenner, and D. H. Bent. 1975. *Statistical Package for the Social Sciences.* New York: McGraw-Hill.

Nunnally, J.C. 1967. *Psychometric Theory.* New York: McGraw-Hill.

Shafer, E. L., Jr., and T. A. Richards. 1974. A comparison of viewer reactions to outdoor scenes and photographs of those scenes. USDA Forest Service Research Paper NE-302, 26 pp. Northeastern Forest Exp. Stn., Broomall, PA.

Shafer, E.L., Jr., J. F. Hamilton, and E. A. Schmidt. 1969. Natural landscape preferences: A predictive model. *Journal of Leisure Research* 1(1): 1–19.

Welsh, G.S. 1966. The perception of our urban environment. *In* R. E. Stipe (Ed.). *Perception and Environment: Foundations of Urban Design.* Chapel Hill: Institute of Government, University of North Carolina.

Wohlwill, J.F. 1968. Amount of stimulus exploration and preference on differential functions of stimulus complexity. *Perception and Psychophysics* 4(5): 307–312.

Wohlwill, J.F., and G. Harris. 1980. Response to congruity or contrast for man-made features in natural recreation settings. *Leisure Sciences* 3(4): 349–365.

Zube, E. 1976. Perception of landscape and land use. *In* I. Altnam and J.E. Wohlwill (Eds.). *Human Behavior and Environment: Advances in Theory and Research* Vol. 1. New York: Plenum Press.

Chapter Three
The Influence of Sociocultural Factors upon Scenic Preferences

Gary D. Hampe
University of Wyoming
Laramie, Wyoming

An individual's scenic preferences are influenced by many things. His culture and society make up just one important part. As is known from previous research on scenic preferences and the more general study of aesthetics, individuals respond simultaneously to the environment around them on several levels (Zube et al., 1975). We know that color, complexity, type of scene, and variety can have an impact on a person physically, emotionally, intellectually, and socially. The relationships between the scenic preferences of visitors and their social background characteristics are examined in this chapter.

The Vista Indices

Five major vistas were found to be typical of the scenes along the Blue Ridge Parkway. These five themes, developed and discussed in depth by Hammitt in Chapter 2, were obtained from factor analyses of the preferences of respondents. Respondents were contacted at three sampling sites along the Blue Ridge Parkway, referred to as the Northern, Middle, and Southern sections.

The number of respondents for each section was as follows: Northern, 241; Middle, 245; Southern, 205. The total sample size was 691.

A total of 96 photographs was used, but only 32 scenes were shown to the respondents in each section. The respondents rated each scene on a scale from one (liked not at all) to five (liked very much). Respondents in each section rated a different set of 32 scenes. The ratings were then factor analyzed within each section, as described in Chapter 2. This resulted in the emergence of five scenic vista types:

1. A Water Vista
2. An Open Multi-Ridged Vista
3. A Developed Vista
4. A One-Ridged Vista
5. An Unmaintained Vista

Indices for each of these vistas were constructed by adding the scores of those scenes that were related to one another on a given factor. (See Hammitt, Chapter 2 for further statistical explanations of the five vistas and rankings of scenes.)

Within each section—Northern, Middle, and Southern—the index for each vista was constructed by adding the rankings given to each picture that had loaded highly on a particular factor: i.e., Open, Unmaintained, One-Ridged, Developed, and Water. The vistas preferred by the respondents from most to least were Water, Open (multi-ridged), Developed (Farm Valley), One-Ridged, and Unmaintained.

The data were analyzed by combining the vistas from the different sections where applicable. Photographs of the Open and Unmaintained Vistas were used in the questionnaires in all three sections of the parkway. One-Ridged Vistas were used in the Northern and Middle sections. Developed Vistas (Farm Valley) were used in Northern and Southern sections, and the Water Vista was measured in the Middle and Southern sections. All the results were checked separately within each of the section subsamples and compared with the results of the total sample. In no case did the relationships change direction. Consistent relationships were found between the dependent variables—the vistas— and the independent variables—the respondents' social background characteristics.

Sociocultural Characteristics of Blue Ridge Parkway Users

The six social background variables obtained were the respondent's age, sex, residence until age 16, educational level, socioeconomic index (occupational SEI), and total (gross) household income. Table 3.1 shows the percentage distributions of these variables for the total sample of all three sections.

The mean age of the respondents was 43.8 years. The distribution of ages varied from 15 to 81. Three age decades, which represented about 60% of the sample, were 30–39, 40–49, and 50–59 (23.6, 21.7, and 19.7%, respectively). For analytical purposes, the respondents were grouped into three age categories of 15–34 (31.0%), 35–54 (40.6%), and 55–81 (28.5%). The respondents in our sample were about 10 years older on the average than the general U.S. population; however, they are considered representative of those 15 years and older in the United States (Bureau of the Census, 1984). Males constituted 71.2% of the sample and females 28.8%. This is, of course, not representative of the general population of the United States, which is slightly over 50% female. However, we already knew that travelers and commuters on a parkway are more likely to be males (Hampe, 1983).

Youthful residence of the respondent was used as an indicator of scenic preference, since previous research has shown that the location of childhood residence influences aesthetic preferences more than recent adult residence (Hampe, 1974). Present residence was also checked to determine if it did make a difference. It did not. The place of residence

Table 3.1. Percentage distributions of respondents for total sample and by six sociocultural background characteristics.

Background Characteristics	Percent	Background Characteristics	Percent
Age		Educational Level	
15 - 34	31.0	Grade School	9.4
35 - 54	40.6	High School	29.2
55 - 82	28.5	Some College	18.9
Total	100.1	College Degree	23.7
(N)	(678)	Advanced Degree	18.8
		Total	100.0
Sex		(N)	(688)
Male	71.2		
Female	28.8	Socioeconomic Index (SEI)	
Total	100.0	Housewife, student, retired	15.0
(N)	(684)	Low (2 -59)	23.2
		Middle (60 - 85)	31.2
Residence		High (86 - 99)	30.7
Country	29.4	Total	100.0
Town	34.2	(N)	(574)
City	36.4		
Total	100.0	Household Income	
(N)	(684)	$0-14,999	19.8
		$15,000-19,999	11.6
		$20,000-29,999	27.2
		$30,000 +	41.4
		Total	100.0
		(N)	(655)

up to age 16 generally reflected the national distribution of the U.S. population. Seventy-four percent of the respondents were from urban areas with populations of 2500 or more, and 26% were from rural areas. The respondents in this sample were about equally distributed among cities (36.4%), towns (34.2%) and country (29.4%). There are a few more individuals from the country in the sample than one would expect by chance, but this is not unexpected when sampling in a rural area such as the Blue Ridge Parkway.

Our sample also proved to be highly educated, with 18.8% having an advanced degree beyond the bachelor's level. Over twenty percent (23.7%) had a bachelor's degree, and 18.9% attended some college. Those with high school and grade school educations (29.2% and 9.4%, respectively) were underrepresented in comparison with the general population. The adult educational level in the United States is just about 12.5 years of education per adult individual.

The high educational levels are reflected in the high income levels of this sample as compared to the general U.S. population (U.S. Bureau of Labor Statistics, 1984). The median household income in the United States is slightly over $21,000 a year. In our sample, 41.4% had a household income of $30,000 or more per year. About one-fifth (19.8%) had a household income of less than $15,000. This latter group consisted of a large number of students and retired individuals.

Our sample of respondents from the Blue Ridge Parkway can thus be characterized as being predominately male, with an early residence evenly distributed among the city, town, and country. They were highly educated, had higher than average income and occupational levels, and were representative of the adult population of the United States only in terms of age.

Interrelationships Between the Sociocultural Background Characteristics

The relationships that exist among the sociocultural background characteristics need to be discussed to understand their effects on vista preferences. The social background characteristics are both directly and indirectly related to one another.

Table 3.2 provides a quick summary of the correlations using Tau (a statistical technique that measures the degree of association between variables). Age was correlated negatively and significantly with education, income, and residence. This is due to the higher educational levels of the younger age cohorts, the effects of education upon the kinds of occupations one can enter, and subsequent income level. Lastly, age was related negatively to residence because of the migration of younger age cohorts to more urban areas. This means that the younger indi-

Table 3.2. Interrelated summary of background variables.

	Tau	Probability of Tau
SEI & Income	−.148	<.001
SEI & Sex	.007	.425
SEI & Residence	.084	.012
SEI & Education	.398	<.001
SEI & Income	.293	<.001
Age & Sex	.006	.437
Age & Residence	−.078	.010
Age & Education	−.069	.020
Age & Income	−.020	.274
Sex & Residence	n.s.	n.s.
Sex & Education	n.s.	n.s.
Sex & Income	−.122	<.001
Residence & Education	.256	<.001
Residence & Income	.118	.004
Education & Income	.280	<.001

Tau refers to strength of the association between the two variables and can vary from −1 (negative relationship) through 0 (no relationship) to +1 (positive relationship). Those relationships which should be recognized as being relatively important are those where the significance level of Tau is less than .05

viduals live in urban areas, while older individuals are more likely to live in rural areas.

Sex of the respondent was correlated significantly with the respondents' annual gross household income. Males were more likely to have higher incomes than females. This relationship reflected the distribution of income by sex for the general population as well. Females on the average earn about 60% of what males earn (Bureau of Labor Statistics, 1984).

Residence of one's youth was positively associated with education, occupational SEI, and income. Those who are more highly educated, in higher occupational levels, and who make more money live in the urban areas of the United States, as contrasted to those living in small towns or in rural areas of the country.

No relationship was found between sex and education, sex and occupational SEI, and sex and residence. No significant relationships were expected.

Our sample of respondents showed strong positive relationships among the variables of education, income and occupational SEI because these variables influence and are dependent upon one another. This was consistent with national surveys. We were then able to generalize to the national level about many of the findings about scenic preferences that are related to the social background characteristics.

The interrelationships of the sociocultural background characteristics are important in understanding the vista preferences of the respondents. When considered separately and in combination, they help to explain some of the variation in the scenic preferences of individuals.

Description and Analysis of Vista Preferences

Open Vista

Those variables which reflect our position in society—educational level, occupational SEI, and income level—were all related significantly to liking or not liking the Open Vista. All three variables were related negatively. That is, the lower the educational level or occupational SEI or income level of the respondent, the more the Open Vista is liked (see Table 3.3). Of those with an advanced degree, 45.3% liked these scenes as compared to 52.0% of those with a high school education and 54.5% of those with a grade school education. Approximately the same distribution of responses was found for the relationship between income and preference for the Open Vista. Finally, scenes of Open Vistas were liked more by the lower social class levels than the higher social class levels.

Age was related positively to liking an Open Vista and was close to being statistically significant ($\chi^2 = 5.807$ and P = .054). Older individuals were more likely to prefer the Open Vistas than were younger individuals by about 10% (51.2% to 41.4%, respectively). This positive relationship is consistent with the negative relationships of those measures of social class, level of education, income and occupational SEI. This is because older individuals in the sample and the general U.S. population have less education and lower income, and often are lower on the occupational SEI as contrasted to the younger individuals today.

Where the respondent was raised until age 16 (residence) was negatively associated (significantly) with preferring the Open Vistas. Those who grew up in the country preferred the Open Vista more (56.3%) than those who grew up in the city (45.9%).

Sex was not significantly related to liking or not liking the scenes of the Open Vista, but as will be seen, sex is an important factor in relationship to the preference of scenes in the other vistas.

The results are consistent between social class levels and preference for the Open Vista. Those who could be classified as members of the working and lower classes prefer the Open Vista scenes more than those of the middle and upper classes. At the same time, it should be kept in mind that this is a high status sample and probably indicates that the users of the parkway are of higher status than the general population. The differences are not overwhelming in the preference of scenes in the Open Vista, but they are consistent. This is important for the individuals who use the parkway.

Table 3.3. Preference for open vista by background characteristics (percent*).

	Degree Like Vista				Degree Like Vista		
	Little	Lot	(N)		Little	Lot	(N)
Age				Where Raised			
15-34	58.6	41.4	(181)	Country	43.7	56.3	(167)
35-54	47.2	52.8	(229)	Town	54.5	45.5	(209)
55-82	48.8	51.2	(170)	City	58.1	45.9	(209)

$X^2 = 5.807$, P = .054, T = .084, P = .031 $X^2 = 5.369$, P = .068, T = .084, P = .031

Sex				SEI			
Male	52.8	47.2	(415)	HSR**	46.4	53.6	(69)
Female	49.4	50.6	(170)	Low	38.4	61.6	(112)
				Mid	57.1	42.9	(154)
				High	54.6	45.4	(152)

$X^2 = .4188$, P = .517; T = .031, P = .230 $X^2 = 10.780$, P = .013; T = -.115, P = .011

Education				Income			
Grade	45.5	54.5	(55)	$1 -14,000	42.2	57.8	(116)
H.S.	48.0	52.0	(171)	$15-19,999	58.1	41.9	(62)
Some coll	50.8	40.2	(120)	$20-29,999	51.3	48.7	(156)
Coll degree	54.7	45.3	(137)	$30,000 +	59.6	45.4	(227)
Adv degree	57.1	42.9	(105)				

$X^2 = 3.603$, P = .462; T = -.088, P = .029 $X^2 = 5.967$, P = .113; T = -.099, P = .015

* The percent is represented by those numbers to the left of the number within the parentheses. Except for a few rounding errors they total 100.0 percent. For example, 58.6 percent of those individuals age 15-34 liked the Open Vista only a "Little." This is 58.6 percent of 181 which represents 105 individuals. Of the 181 individuals age 15-34, 41.4 percent liked the Open Vista a "Lot."
** HSR refers to housewives, students and retired individuals in this and the following tables in this chapter.

Unmaintained Vista

Sex was the most statistically significant variable in differentiating preferences of scenes comprising the Unmaintained Vista. Women were more likely to prefer the Unmaintained Vista (58.4%) than the men (46.2%, P = .008); see Table 3.4.

There were two other relationships where both chi square and Tau were statistically significant. Individuals who were raised in the country preferred Unmaintained Vistas (58.6%) more than those who were raised in the city (49.1%). Those who were raised in towns liked the Unmaintained Vistas least (44.4%).

The three measures of social class—education, occupational SEI, and income—were all related negatively to the Unmaintained Vista index. The Taus were all statistically significant.

Table 3.4. Preference for unmaintained vista by background characteristics (percent).

	Degree Like Vista				Degree Like Vista		
	Little	Lot	(N)		Little	Lot	(N)
Age				SEI			
15-34	55.3	44.7	(190)	HSR	50.7	49.3	(73)
35-54	47.1	52.9	(240)	Low	39.5	60.3	(114)
55-82	47.1	52.3	(172)	Mod	54.8	45.2	(157)
				High	51.3	48.7	(158)

$X^2 = 3.287$, P = .193; T = .065, P = .068 $X^2 = 6.751$, P = .080; T = .058, P = .118

	Degree Like Vista				Degree Like Vista		
	Little	Lot	(N)		Little	Lot	(N)
Education				Sex			
Grade	42.6	57.4	(54)	Male	53.8	46.2	(433)
H.S.	46.7	53.3	(180)	Female	41.6	58.4	(173)
Some Coll	50.4	49.6	(121)				
Coll Degree	52.9	47.1	(140)				
Adv. Degree	55.3	44.7	(114)				

$X^2 = 3.712$, P = .446; T = .087, P = .028 $X^2 = 6.870$, P = .009; T = .099, P = .003

	Degree Like Vista				Degree Like Vista		
	Little	Lot	(N)		Little	Lot	(N)
Income				Where Raised			
$1 -14,999	40.3	59.7	(119)	Country	41.4	58.6	(174)
$15-19,999	49.2	50.8	(63)	Town	55.6	44.4	(216)
$20-29,999	51.6	48.4	(159)	City	50.9	49.1	(216)
$30,000 +	53.7	46.2	(240)				

$X^2 = 5.966$, P = .113; T = .099, P = .014 $X^2 = 11.035$, P = .019; T = -.074, P = .048

The overall pattern of the relationships of the sociocultural background characteristics was consistent and in the same direction as found for the Open Vista. The only notable significant difference was with the females preferring the Unmaintained Vista more than did the males.

One-Ridged Vista

The results shown in Table 3.5 indicate that the relationships between preferences for the One-Ridged Vista and the socio-cultural background characteristics are consistent with the findings for the Open and Unmaintained Vistas. One of the relationships not statistically significant but still in the same direction as the previous ones is between sex and the One-Ridged Vista. Females were more likely to like these scenes very much (37.5%) as compared to males (28.4%).

Briefly summarizing the significant relationships, we found that those who liked the One-Ridged Vista more were those who had lower occupational SEI scores, were from lower educational levels, had lower income levels, grew up in the country, and were older. They liked this

Table 3.5. Preference for one ridge vista by background characteristics (percent).

	Degree Like Vista					Degree Like Vista			
	Little	Mod	Lot	(N)		Little	Mod	Lot	(N)
Age					SEI				
15-34	38.5	33.1	28.5	(130)	HSR	28.3	43.3	28.3	(60)
25-54	31.7	34.4	33.4	(186)	Low	23.3	37.9	41.9	(86)
55-82	46.2	33.4	31.1	(132)	Mod	34.8	34.8	30.4	(115)
					High	38.2	34.1	27.6	(123)

$X^2 = 9.820$, P = .043; T = .077, P = .032 $X^2 = 8.816$, P = .184; T = -.087, P = .029

Where Raised					Sex				
Country	25.0	32.0	43.0	(128)	Male	33.8	37.7	28.4	(334)
Town	32.7	40.6	26.7	(165)	Female	25.8	36.7	37.5	(120)
City	35.0	38.7	26.2	(160)					

$X^2 = 11.981$, P = .018; T = .113, P = .003 $X^2 = 4.155$, P = .125; T = .041, P = .021

Education					Income				
Grade	13.2	42.1	44.7	(38)	$1 -14,999	20.8	37.7	41.6	(77)
H.S.	26.2	35.4	38.5	(130)	$15-19,999	27.3	38.6	34.1	(44)
Some Coll	33.0	42.9	24.2	(91)	$20-29,999	27.9	45.7	26.4	(129)
Coll Degree	36.3	40.2	23.5	(102)	$30,000 +	39.1	31.5	29.3	(184)
Adv. Degree	40.0	29.5	30.5	(95)					

$X^2 = 18.923$, P = .015; T = -.142, P<.001 $X^2 = 15.066$, P = .018; T = .120, P = .002

type of vista from 10 to 40% more than those who rated higher on the social class measures and those who were younger.

Developed Vista

The consistency of the relationships of the sociocultural background characteristics is again seen in the preference of the respondents for the Developed Vista (see Table 3.6). The most statistically significant variable (according to both the chi square and Tau analyses) was the relationship between educational level and the Developed Vista index. The lower the educational level of the respondents, the more likely they were to like a vista with some type of building in the view. Grade school- and high school-educated respondents were more likely to prefer this type of scene than the college-educated (48.4 and 44.1 to 28.7%, respectively).

The relationships were weaker, but with statistically significant Taus, between the Developed Vista index and youthful residence, occupational SEI, and sex. Again, as with the other vista indices, the Developed Vista was preferred more by those reared in the country, those of

Table 3.6. Preference for developed vista by background characteristics (percent).

	Degree Like Vista					Degree Like Vista			
	Little	Mod	Lot	(N)		Little	Mod	Lot	(N)
Age					Where Raised				
15-34	28.1	36.7	35.2	(168)	Country	25.9	31.0	43.1	(116)
35-54	30.0	31.9	38.1	(160)	Town	33.1	34.6	32.4	(136)
55-82	27.4	31.3	31.3	(115)	City	35.3	33.3	31.4	(156)

$X^2 = 3.412$, P = .481; T = -.052, P = .118 $X^2 = 5.196$, P = .267; T = -.088, P = .023

Sex					SEI				
Male	35.2	31.4	33.4	(290)	HSR	25.6	25.6	48.8	(43)
Female	23.7	26.4	39.8	(118)	Low	25.3	36.7	38.0	(79)
					Mod	32.7	38.5	28.8	(104)
					High	35.1	30.7	34.2	(114)

$X^2 = 5.069$, P = .079; T = .097, P = .024 $X^2 = 7.653$, P = .265; T = -.089, P = .037

Education					Income				
Grade	19.4	32.3	48.4	(31)	$1 -14,000	23.1	33.3	43.6	(78)
H.S.	22.0	33.9	44.1	(118)	$15-19,999	42.6	31.5	25.9	(54)
Some Coll	36.1	34.9	29.9	(83)	$20-29,999	34.7	29.5	35.9	(95)
Coll Degree	34.0	37.2	28.7	(94)	$30,000 +	31.7	34.2	34.2	(161)
Adv. Degree	43.9	25.6	30.5	(82)					

$X^2 = 18.200$, P = .019; T = -.163, P = <.001 $X^2 = 7.394$, P = .285; T = -.032, P = .235

lower occupational SEI, and by females. A curvilinear relationship between age and the Developed Vista was found with those in the middle-aged category (age 35–54) preferring the Developed Vista more than those at the younger and older ends of the age continuum (38.1 to 35.2 and 31.3%, respectively). A curvilinear relationship was also found to exist with income. Those at the lower and upper ends of the income continuum were more likely to prefer the Developed Vista than those in the middle categories, but the differences were not statistically significant.

Finally, those from the lower social class levels were more likely to prefer the Developed Vista than those from the upper levels. It should be pointed out that 33 to 40% of those in the higher social classes, as measured by education, income, and occupational SEI, definitely did not like the Developed Vista.

Water Vista

The Water Vista, which was composed of both fast-moving and still scenes of water, was preferred significantly by more females (37.3%)

Table 3.7. Preference for water vista by background characteristics (percent).

	Degree Like Vista					Degree Like Vista			
	Little	Mod	Lot	(N)		Little	Mod	Lot	(N)
Age					Where Raised				
15-34	11.8	57.4	30.9	(136)	Country	12.7	51.6	35.7	(124)
35-54	14.5	50.3	35.2	(165)	Town	16.0	51.3	32.7	(150)
55-82	17.8	48.3	33.9	(118)	City	13.9	54.2	31.9	(144)

$X^2 = 3.147$, P = .533, T = -.007, P = .427 $\qquad$ $X^2 = 0.998$, P = .910; T = -.024, P = .274

	Little	Mod	Lot	(N)		Little	Mod	Lot	(N)
Sex					SEI				
Male	17.5	51.9	30.5	(285)	H/S/R	14.3	51.8	33.9	(54)
Female	9.0	53.7	37.3	(134)	Low	11.8	43.5	44.7	(85)
					Mod	20.8	54.7	24.5	(106)
					High	16.2	49.5	34.3	(99)

$X^2 = 5.884$, P = .052, T = .100, P = .017 $\qquad$ $X^2 = 9.436$, P = .150; T = -.053, P = .132

	Little	Mod	Lot	(N)		Little	Mod	Lot	(N)
Education					Income				
Grade	5.8	55.8	38.5	(52)	$1 -14,999	4.3	57.4	38.3	(94)
H.S.	14.0	53.5	32.6	(129)	$15-19,999	21.4	40.5	38.1	(42)
Some Coll	15.5	49.3	35.2	(71)	$20-29,999	14.3	56.3	29.5	(112)
Coll Degree	18.3	51.0	30.8	(104)	$30,000 +	20.4	51.6	28.0	(157)
Adv. Degree	16.4	52.2	31.3	(67)					

$X^2 = 5.052$, P = .752; T = -.058, P = .085 $\qquad$ $X^2 = 15.948$, P = .014; T = -.118, P = .003

than by males (30.5%) (see Table 3.7). Also statistically significant for both chi square and Tau was the relationship with income. Those of the lower income levels were more likely to prefer the Water Vista (38.3 and 38.1%, respectively) than those of the higher income levels (29.5 and 28.0%, respectively).

Although the relationships of the Water Vista with age, youthful residence, educational level, or occupational SEI were not statistically significant, each relationship was consistent with the findings for the other vistas. The lower social class levels again preferred this vista more than the higher social class levels.

What is most noticeable about the preferences of the respondents for the Water Vista is the large proportion of individuals who are moderate in their preference for this particular vista. At least 50 percent of all the respondents moderately liked the Water Vista, regardless of their sociocultural background. This distribution sharply contrasts with that found for the One-Ridged and Developed Vistas, which were also constructed and analyzed as trichotomies. On the whole, only a very small proportion of the respondents did not like the Water Vista. Also, most respondents were much more likely to prefer this vista than any of the other vistas. (For more specific information, see the rankings of the individual scenes and the sub-types of vistas as delineated by Hammitt in Chapter 2).

Explanation and Prediction of the Five Vistas

Stepwise regression was performed on each of the five vista indices to determine how much of the variation of ranking scenes was explained by the six sociocultural background characteristics. Table 3.8 shows the three most important variables for predicting and explaining the choice of each vista index. Several important findings can be derived from these results. First, the proportion of variance (Multiple R-squared) explained by the independent variables is quite low, ranging from about 3 to 5% of the variation. Socio-cultural background characteristics, then, are not the main explanatory factors in the determination of vista preferences, at least for this sample of respondents and set of scenic vistas. However, it is helpful to know what types of individuals are most likely to use the Blue Ridge Parkway. The background differences of users do influence how individuals differentiate among the scenes they encounter and how much they like or do not like various types of scenes.

From a superficial as well as an intensive look at the 96 scenes, it is obvious that there is not much variety in the basic landscape forms that are being compared. This, along with the great number of choices (32 to each group of respondents at each data-gathering site), would decrease the possibility of explaining a great deal of variation of the dependent variables. If we compare the results from other research sites and studies of aesthetic preferences, the lack of a high percentage of explanation is not surprising (See Hampe, 1974, 1983; Zube, et al.,1975).

A second important finding from the regression analysis is the consistency of the importance of three background characteristics—sex, income and youthful residence—for the five vistas. From the cross-classification analysis, the respondent's sex was most often statistically significant and also showed the greatest percentage difference between categories. The same was true, but to a lesser extent, for income level and youthful residence.

Summary

The sociocultural background characteristics of the respondents were examined in relation to their preferences for the five vista indices— Open, Unmaintained, One-Ridged, Developed, and Water. They were found to differentiate between groups on the degree individuals pre-

Table 3.8. The five vistas by the three most important variables for each (stepwise regression).

			Open Vista			
Independent Variables	R^2	r	Beta	P(Beta)	F	P(F)*
Occupation - SEI	.109	−.109	−.095	.070	5.814	.016
Sex	.143	.089	.089	.051	5.050	.007
Where Raised	.153	−.084	−.067	.157	4.108	.007

$R^2 = .025$, $F = 4.108$, $P = .007$

			Unmaintained Vista			
Sex	.131	.132	.122	.007	8.553	.004
Income	.166	−.119	−.074	.134	6.917	.001
Where Raised	.181	−.086	−.063	.177	5.500	.001

$R^2 = .033$, $F = 5.497$, $P = .001$

			Developed Vista			
Education	.181	−.181	−.147	.023	11.393	.001
Sex	.198	.099	.093	.093	6.858	.001
Age	.210	−.063	−.077	.077	5.165	.002

$R^2 = .044$, $F = 5.156$, $P = .002$

			One-Ridged Vista			
Income	.157	−.157	−.095	.107	9.374	.002
Sex	.192	.116	.102	.046	7.143	.001
Occupation & SEI	.217	−.136	−.094	.074	<6.121	<.001

$R^2 = .047$, $F = 6.121$, $P < .001$

			Water Vista			
Income	.149	−.149	−.101	.082	7.757	.006
Sex	.184	.128	.115	.032	6.017	.003
Occupation & SEI	.192	−.089	−.078	.211	4.360	.005

$R^2 = .037$, $F = 4.360$, $P = .005$

*R^2 is multiple R squared, r is the correlation coefficient, P(Beta) is the probability Beta and P(F) is the probability of the F ratio.

ferred or did not prefer a particular vista. The consistency of preferring or not preferring the vistas was nothing short of remarkable.

This consistency was due in part to the lack of variety among the basic landforms of the different scenes (see Hampe and Noe, 1980; Zube, 1973). It can be stated that those individuals of the lower class levels, females, and the older persons like the open views along the

Blue Ridge more than individuals who were of higher social class levels, males, and the younger persons. Further work needs to be done to determine why these groups liked or disliked these vistas.

In particular, we need to ask more questions about why a particular view is popular or unpopular. Is it the trees, the mountains, the water, the shrubs, the clouds, the color? Also, we need to consider the complexity and variety of the views, the reasons for the trip, what one does during a trip (driving or not driving), the individual's personal environmental concerns, and so on. Additional research in these areas would prove valuable in further understanding the aesthetic experiences of individuals who use the Blue Ridge.

REFERENCES

Bureau of Labor Statistics. 1984. U. S. Dept. of Labor, Washington, D.C. U. S. Gov. Printing Office, January 10, p. 84–85.

Hampe, G. D. 1974. *Water-related Aesthetic Preferences of Wyoming Residents*. Univ. of Wyoming, Laramie, WY.

Hampe, G. D. 1983. Final report on the parameters of sightseeing experiences of individuals along parkways and the effects upon scenic preferences. Univ. of Wyoming, Laramie, WY.

Hampe, G. D., and F. P. Noe. 1980. Visual complexity and preference for parkway scenes. *Perceptual and Motor Skills* 51:587–592.

U. S. Bureau of the Census. 1984. Statistical Abstract of the United States. Edition 105, Washington, D.C.

Zube, E. H. 1973. Rating everyday rural landscapes of the northeastern U.S. *Landscape Architecture* July:371–374.

Zube, E. H., D. G. Pitt, and T. W. Anderson. 1975. Perception and prediction of scenic resource values of the northeast. *In Landscape Assessment Values, Perceptions, and Resources*. E. H. Zube, R. O. Brush, and J. Fabos (eds.). Stroudsburg, PA: Dowden, Hutchinson, and Ross.

Chapter Four
Effects of Recreational and Environmental Values on Tourists' Scenic Preferences

Francis P. Noe
National Park Service
Southeast Regional Office
Atlanta, Georgia

Modern road builders and engineers, like their counterparts in ancient Rome, have made value judgements about the social utility of their designs. The ancient Romans built straight roads on high ground with no curves or bends to help the marching legions avoid ambush. Modern civil engineers have designed multi-lane expressways to accommodate legions of trucks and autos and facilitate the commercial link for moving goods and materials. As a result, the American highway system has influenced the development of large urban commercial centers and has brought progress to rural areas and made our nation more accessible to travel and trade.

Besides the pragmatic economic objectives that are obviously accomplished by roads, less materialistic benefits are also achieved through the aesthetic design of roadways. Although an aesthetic experience may be less important than more practical needs, the pleasure of driving is measurably enhanced by parkways designed to improve the aesthetic quality of life. The Blue Ridge Parkway, for example, was established as a connection between the Shenandoah and Great Smoky Mountains National Parks to showcase the beauty and cultural lifestyle of the region to the motoring public.

How do public values and attitudes about the environment and recreation affect the appreciation of a roadway ostensibly designed for touring? At the Blue Ridge Parkway, the motoring public is exposed to a widely diverse environment that stimulates visual judgments. It takes "all of our (their) sensory experiences" to make those judgments (Buhyoff, et al., 1978). "It is important to recognize, however, that the landscape's values include more than preferences. A landscape may be valued by an individual in the sense that he or she likes it, or likes it better than others—thus the study of values as preferences. But it may also be valued by a society or culture whether or not a particular individual or group prefers it" (Andrews, 1979). Regardless of who is judging the value of the environment, "various scholars have argued that perception is an integral part of individual and group dynamics" (Rose, 1975). While both the individual and the group make acceptable judges, the research described in this chapter focuses on individual perceptions.

Value Orientations

Two commonly held values influencing the scenic judgments of individuals are thought to be their beliefs toward (1) nature and the rural environments and (2) leisure and recreation. In defining values relating to the environment, three variations have been offered as explanations. These are (a) *preference*, which relates to matters of individual taste (i.e., I like sightseeing better than hunting); (b) *obligatory*, which relates to group-shared norms (i.e., Do not start forest fires through neglect); and (c) *functional*, which refers to the known relationships in nature that produce benefits for mankind (i.e., Soil conservation saves streams and rivers). These three definitions represent what social scientists call attitudinal, normative, and cognitive beliefs, respectively. Attitudinal beliefs (i.e. the preference definition) are the subject of our research in this chapter.

A recent explanation of how values or attitudinal beliefs influence preferences is in the Stanford Research Institute's studies of values and lifestyles (Mitchell, 1983). That research began with "the premise that an individual's array of inner values would create specific matching patterns of outer behavior—that is, of lifestyles" (Mitchell, 1983). In essence, an individual's beliefs support certain lifestyle tastes. Our adaptation of the concept of values to the study of aesthetic evaluation in this chapter assumes that beliefs promote certain tastes that the tourists apply to scenes along a roadway. Values can help determine why tourists prefer particular scenic views along the Blue Ridge Parkway.

Perhaps the most effective way to present our research on the relationship between the tourists' attitudinal beliefs and values and their scenic preferences is to describe some of the previous research conducted in that field.

Natural Environmental Values

If a person decides to tour the Blue Ridge Parkway, his beliefs about the scenic value of nature and the environment may be a part of his motivation. In analyzing the results of an environmental preference questionnaire, Kaplan (1977) found that "the person who seeks natural settings whenever possible, including when under stress, favors activities which permit expression of the preferences. Thus, he chooses activities when he can find out about things in nature." Seeking knowledge about nature through learning and deciding to visit places of natural beauty help strengthen a set of beliefs. An underlying pattern of socialization is likely to exist among parkway tourists who share a positive orientation for the natural setting. The findings of the North Atlantic Regional Water Resource Study, which summarized projects on seven different sample groups of landscape professionals, students, and adults, demonstrated a pattern of preference for the natural over the man-made scene. "When the landscapes were predominantly natural or consisted of natural material such as in agricultural areas . . . the predicted rank order evaluations correlated moderately to highly with the rank orders of the seven participant subgroups" (Zube et al., 1975). Whatever the reasons for choosing the natural over the man-made, the natural scene received a higher value.

The extent to which a tendency toward the natural exists throughout history is debatable and not easily identified. Some scholars believe that the natural perspective is an "aesthetic aberration in the history of landscape taste. . . . In most canons of landscape beauty, man and his works occupy a prominent place" (Lowenthal, 1962–3). Whether at some point in history, cultures will again shift preferences to the man-made, no one is willing to venture a guess. For now, at least, "men do indeed view natural objects in ways distinct from artificial objects" (Kates, 1966–7). These differences account for the acceptance and enjoyment as well as rejection and disdain of various landscape scenes.

Studies manipulating the amount and levels of human interference using photo representation techniques of natural situations further tested the strength of preferences for man-made over purely natural scenes. The landscape scenes were quantitatively varied by the number and presence of people or man-made structures to measure their effect on landscape preferences. The results of these studies indicate "that preference tends to decrease as the levels of people and development increase" (Carls, 1974). If scenes in nature are preferred, then they will probably contain few signs of man-made structural modification. While the man-made scene gives way to the natural scenes in preference, how are scenic choices influenced by the recreational preferences of individuals? We will explore this question in the following section.

Outdoor Recreation Values

Preferences for outdoor recreation activities have been the subject of increased investigation during the past two decades. Many of these studies classified individual activities into more general categories. For example, individual activities such as hiking, walking, and sightseeing were classified as appreciative recreation, while hunting and fishing were classified as consumptive recreation. However, many of these classification schemes were not always tested beyond a preliminary inquiry, and most suffered from a lack of scientific replication. Despite these problems, progress has been made toward recognizing the similarities among recreational activities.

Treating a class of recreational activities as a more general category started with preference studies. These studies supported the observation that "individuals tend to engage in a set of activities rather than one particular pursuit" (Noe et al., 1981). Individuals tend to prefer similar kinds of activities and exclude others from their consideration. In one relatively large study, "the results of the analysis indicated the degree to which people are more likely to take part in several activities within a given group of activities than to take part in those activities which fall into different groups" (Yeosting et al., 1973). In general, recreational behavior is not random behavior, and recreational activities are organized into classes of similar behavior which may also have an influence on scenic preferences.

Research was then conducted to determine if visual preferences for a parkway landscape were related to recreational classes of activity (Noe et al., 1981). The researchers found that tourists engaging in "passive outdoor experiences" have a greater liking for less manicured parkway scenes, while those who do not participate in passive outdoor activities are less likely to appreciate the natural beauty of the parkway. Passive outdoor recreation generally refers to activities that require little physical exertion, such as sightseeing, learning, and viewing visitor demonstrations. In contrast, tourists who pursue "active outdoor experiences" that require team effort and physical skill prefer a roadway scene where the vegetation is mowed and manicured. Less maintained scenes were disliked by those recreationists engaged in active sports like tennis and bicycling, which require individual skill and effort (Noe et al., 1981).

Outdoor recreational activities are often associated with "places where individuals can relax, play, engage in physical activity, get away from urban pleasures, return to nature, seek solitude, and so on"

(Berry, 1976). A need for such places predisposes the public to be more receptive to environmental conditions. As a result, the protection of landscapes is often motivated by the contemplative and aesthetic values of individuals. Believing that open space is beautiful has led to recognizing that more "passive forms of recreation" are also of "relatively great importance" (Berry, 1976). Outdoor sites are valued for being quiet, peaceful, and natural as well as offering opportunities for walks among trees and affording areas containing few people. The recreationist not only defines beauty in terms of a physical environment but also finds activities like passive recreation (i.e., sightseeing) compatible with appreciating the beauty of nature.

Visual qualities characterizing a landscape as "clean, hilly, tree-studded, grassy, pleasant, beautiful, natural, green, peaceful, and sunny" were also associated with a wide range of leisure activities other than just passive types (Craik, 1975). Those individuals who found it difficult to characterize the landscape belonged to fewer service, community, and religious organizations, read fewer magazines, did not participate in homecraft or glamour sports (archery, horseback riding, and water-skiing), and did not support land being used for state parks. Those individuals who were able to more easily characterize the landscape belonged to a larger number of organizations, including ecological and conservation groups, and were devoted to neighborhood sports and mechanical pursuits (i.e., hobbies such as tinkering with cars, woodworking, fixing appliances, etc.). Heightened recreational use increases our facility to make visual assessments more adroitly.

Recreational experiences also alter tourists' perceptions of the environment. In a study that asked the question, "Do different recreationists perceive the natural environment in the same way?", no simple answer was found; the researchers eventually concluded that "the perception of elements in the natural surrounding depends on the kind of experience a particular recreationist group is seeking and the way in which elements of the natural surroundings enhance or detract from their experiences" (Moeller et al., 1974). For example, auto campers, wilderness hikers, and picnickers perceived their environment as more valuable than did other groups. The specialization that frequently occurs in recreational activities heightens the awareness of the value of certain site characteristics. Obviously, the more favorable a site is for an activity, the more popular and desirable it will be to that recreationist. In most instances the natural environment is favorably rated by outdoor recreational groups (Moeller et al., 1974).

Previous visual assessment studies have placed undue emphasis on a physical situation like a roadway rather than on the respondents' recreational experiences. Zube et al. (1984) found that the current trend in research is to place little emphasis on social, psychological, and recreative behavior. Most research tends to follow a behavioralist approach stressing landscape properties (stimulus) over the respondent (response). One widely followed model explains scenic attractiveness by identifying site characteristics associated with scenes in nature (Shafer et al., 1969). The site preferences of "campers" in the Adirondacks were defined by a certain proportion of vegetation, sky, lakes, waterfalls, and nonvegetation. While "camper" site preferences were explained, their recreational experiences were not explored.

Even today, the lack of knowledge about recreational experiences hampers management's understanding of how recreationists view their surroundings. In particular, studies narrowly dealing with site characteristics are criticized since they ignore recreational experiences in site assessment and evaluation. The importance of recreational values offers another potential explanation for predicting scenic preferences.

Blue Ridge Parkway Findings

The recreational, environmental, and scenic values of parkway tourists were tested and analyzed regarding their preferences toward scenes on the Blue Ridge Parkway. The tourists' frequency of visiting the parkway was also measured. Two indicators were applied to measure the level of the tourists' sightseeing involvement: stopping at overlooks and taking photographs. The number of photographs taken and the frequency of stopping appear to be related to the tourists' scenic preferences.

This analysis will concentrate only on those scenes that managers can control. Those overlooks containing vegetation that can obstruct or alter views are high priority. Factor and Alpha analysis techniques were used to locate points of similarity and dissimilarity among scenes and to discover the potential agreement of respondents among various pictorial scenes. As described by Hammitt in Chapter 2, two clusters of scenes tended to be most similar and dissimilar in their interrelationship: (1) unmaintained, vegetated vista scenes, which were the most disliked, and (2) open, multi-ridged scenes, which were highly liked by tourists. Differences in value orientations were measured against preferences for the open and unmaintained scenes.

Frequency of Stopping and Photographing

We found a positive and direct relationship between the amount of stopping and the number of photographs taken. Because stopping and photographing are interrelated, we combined both of these indicators into a single measure. The results show greater participation than we first expected. The majority of tourists felt they needed to pull off, stop, and leave their vehicle to have an adequate sightseeing experience. Thirty-four percent of the tourists stopped between five and 15 times along the parkway. Another 30% stopped between one and five times. Conversely, 34% felt no need to stop to appreciate the scenery, while the remaining 2% were undecided. To discount as trivial the pull-offs and scenic vistas that allow visitors to stop and enjoy the rural landscape scenes would be an obvious miscalculation of a tourist attraction. Quite clearly, the visitors use these facilities to maximize their experience.

The number of photographs taken by the tourists indicates an effort to commemorate their visit, which they can share with their friends and family, as well as to vicariously relive for themselves. Among those tourists who stopped along the parkway and took photographs, 60% took at least one photo, and 26% of that group took between 11 and 36 or more photos. However, 40% did not take any photographs of the parkway.

Clearly, to take photographs is a dominant experience for many of the visitors. These tourists are not merely sitting behind the wheel of a vehicle and looking out the windshield. Instead, they are enjoying a sightseeing experience by participating.

Repeat Visits

To control for first-time visitors, tourists were asked about the number of visits that they had made in the past (See Appendix A). The repeat tourists became qualitatively selective in the photographs they took and where they stopped. In general, the number of photographs taken decreased as the number of repeat visits increased, and the frequency of stopping at pull-offs diminished to an average of about five stops per trip. As tourists increased their repeat visitation from one to 10 times or more in a five-year period, they reduced their photography to just a few pictures, except for approximately 26% of those repeat visitors, who still took 11 or more photos. This same group also stopped the most. The amount and intensity of use exhibited by this group do not appear to diminish its enthusiasm and commitment to the Blue Ridge experience.

First-time visitors constituted 32% of our sample, while the remaining 68% were repeat visitors. The repeat visitors generally made fewer stops and took fewer photographs. In contrast, the first-time visitors were the most frequent stoppers and the most prolific photographers. Clearly, the repeat tourists are a significant majority. Given the data on the repeat visitors—i.e., their frequency of stopping and photographing—we now have a better picture of the kind of experience that a majority of those visiting the parkway call "sightseeing." That experience is highly participatory and includes certain attitudes, as we shall see.

Highway Values and Attitudes of Tourists

In a series of environmental questions seeking to explore an individual's orientation to nature, the earth, and roadways (see Appendix A), two attitudinal items related to highways stood out. The possibility of feelings toward roadways was analyzed to determine if such beliefs had anything to do with the way tourists stopped or took photographs. Since the Blue Ridge Parkway represents a different mode of transportation, we hypothesized that people who did not like ordinary highways would be among the more prolific photographers and visitors. This hypothesis proved true. Tourists with negative feelings toward ordinary highways (i.e., considering them to be uninviting and similar looking) took more photographs and stopped more frequently on the parkway than those who had a positive attitude toward highways. The tourists who disliked ordinary highways made up the majority of parkway users (over 60%). Those tourists were not just interested in a good roadway but believed it was possible to enjoy a car-touring experience. They seem to share an ideology that looks beyond the simply pragmatic, utilitarian need to move between two points in a vehicle.

This finding does not indicate a casual experience, but rather one that involves a considerable undertaking. Most of the people in this group stopped about 15 times. These tourists felt that highways are pretty dull, and almost everything looks the same along them. In contrast to the ordinary highway, the Blue Ridge Parkway offers the tourist another option.

In the data analyzed so far, we have focused upon the tourists and their level of participation. That level is surprisingly high with respect to the number of repeat tourists. Since our analysis attempts to discover what attracts tourists, we need to measure how the tourist feels about certain scenes along the Blue Ridge Parkway.

Disliked scenes contain a high degree of vegetation overgrowth and provide an unmaintained view of a vista. These "unmaintained vegetated scenes" are exemplified by a photo in Figure 4.1. Regardless of their location along the parkway, the unmaintained vegetated scenes were identified by tourists as a singular visual experience. They also happened to be the least preferred of the scenes along the Blue Ridge Parkway. At the most preferred end of the scale, a series of photographs depicting an open, multi-ridged vista, as exemplified in Figure 4.2, reveals a relatively free and open perspective to a distant view. Tourists liking a view from an open vista, with its ridges, mountains and cliffs, share a belief that most ordinary highways are generally not good for sightseeing. Conversely, tourists unimpressed with the scenic perspectives of an open vista preferred the practical utility of a highway that primarily serves as a transportation conduit.

The relationship between tourists sharing either a positive or a negative attitude toward highways and their preference for unmaintained

Figure 4.1.   An example of an unmaintained vegetated vista.

Figure 4.2.   An example of an open multi-ridged vista.

scenes was also tested. These tests proved to be statistically insignificant. The belief in highways having a social utility but not a scenic value is perhaps more important for discriminating preferences among tourists for the more desirable rather than the least desirable vistas. While beliefs or attitudes toward a highway may not influence what tourists dislike, they do affect what tourists like.

Environmental Values and Attitudes of Tourists

In the past, the National Environmental Paradigm scale (NEP) has been used to measure the public's concern for the environment. Does a concern for the environment affect attitudes toward highways and scenery?

The NEP scale consists of 12 questions that reflect an individual's concern for nature and man's relationship with the environment (Dunlap et al., 1978). The scale explores the themes of exploitation, dominance, and disrespect for nature as opposed to living in harmony with nature without undue human interference. In adopting the NEP scale to our study, we evaluated it to determine if all the twelve items were needed. An internal reliability check of the scale was run to see if the items formed a singular dimension. Factor and Alpha analyses were performed on the data at this stage to determine precisely the most significant environmental items comprising a reliable set of scores. As a result, a modified version of the NEP scale specifying six questions was adopted (Table 4.1.).

Two attitudinal possibilities could result, depending upon whether a person agreed or disagreed with the scale. If a person agreed with the six scale items, he supported ecological harmony; but if he disagreed, it meant he was more apt to interfere with nature. How do these opposing attitudes reflect a person's aesthetic evaluation of scenes along the Blue Ridge Parkway? If the earlier literature review accurately reflects reality, then environmental attitudes should have some bearing upon a tourist's view of the environment. We found that tourists who believe that man should interfere with the natural environment to suit his needs dislike open vistas reflecting distant ridges, mountains, and far-off panoramas. Tourists believing that man must live in harmony with nature to survive prefer the open vistas that show natural ridgelines, mountains, and distant views. This association between environmental attitudes and preference for open vistas was statistically significant, as indicated by the Chi Square values ($\chi^2 = 10.32$, df $= 1$, P $= .001$).

A significant relationship was also evident for the unmaintained scenes ($\chi^2 = 11.58$, df $= 1$, P $= .001$). Tourists who believe in interfering with the environment did not like an unmaintained scene, while those who believed in living in harmony with nature felt the unmaintained scene had some value. There was a greater tolerance for unmaintained scenes among the latter. Consequently, the manager may either

Table 4.1. Modified NEP Environmental Scale*

Item	Factor Score	Alpha Value
The balance of nature is very delicate and easily upset.	.45	——
Humans have the right to modify the natural environment to suit their needs.	.35	——
When humans interfere with nature it often produces disastrous consequences.	.54	——
To maintain a healthy economy, we will have to develop a "steady-state" economy where industrial growth is controlled.	.37	——
Humans must live in harmony with nature in order to survive.	.47	——
Mankind is severely abusing the environment.	.53	——
	2.43 Eigenvalue	0.64 Total

* Dunlap and Van Liere (1978).

maintain an open vista or allow the vista to be obscured by vegetation. It matters little for those tourists who believe in living harmoniously with nature since they like both types of scenes. Presented with the choice of maintaining both open and partially obscured vistas, the manager could hardly err in satisfying this type of visitor. That the other tourist group cares little for either open or unmaintained vistas helps the manager simply direct his efforts toward satisfying those who express a preference for both types of vistas.

The extent to which vegetation should be allowed to obscure the scene is certainly a question for management to address. Since more tourists prefer the open vista, the most significant ones should be identified. Beyond that, to overstress the importance of the open vista as opposed to the unmaintained may be a disservice to those who like both types. However, the more correct position for management to take would be to emphasize the open vista at the expense of an unmaintained vista.

This information is intended to give the manager more insight into the tourist who possesses important environmental attitudes that are related to visual experiences. A manager might easily follow a recommendation of preserving open vistas but not worry too much about vistas that are obscured since most of the tourists like both. The challenge is in controlling the proper mix of open and unmaintained vistas before the manager loses the support those who prefer both types of vistas.

Recreational Values of Tourists

Some tourists may have specific recreational value expectations for visiting the parkway. Consideration must be given to the individual's specific intentions, whether it is to participate in active recreation or simply to view the scenery. Reasons for using the parkway may also be more practical, such as commuting to work or visiting friends and relatives. A series of eight questions probing a tourist's intentions for visiting the parkway proved quite successful in distinguishing expectations (see Appendix A).

The dominant reason tourists gave for visiting the parkway was for recreation, such as going on a vacation, viewing the scenery, visiting park facilities, and learning more about the area. Visiting friends and relatives or going to and from work were not important to the tourist; neither was participation in active outdoor recreational activities, such as camping, hiking, and picnicking. The predominant expectation is clearly that of obtaining a rewarding sightseeing experience during a visit.

However, do recreational expectations influence parkway participation (measured by photo-taking and stopping) as well as vista preferences? Indeed, significant relationships were found regarding the frequency of photo-taking and the number of times a tourist stopped. Expecting a recreational sightseeing experience was very important for stopping more frequently along the Blue Ridge Parkway ($\chi^2 = 33.14$, df = 3, P = .001) and taking more photographs ($\chi^2 = 30.35$, df = 3, P = .001). The reverse was true for those who did not seek this passive type of recreational experience; they stopped less frequently and took far fewer photos.

Most tourists, then, visited the parkway for a scenic, informed vacation involving themselves in extensive stopping and photography. We now are able to say that not only are these tourists stopping and taking photos, but they are doing so because their reasons are associated with expectations of learning about the Blue Ridge, experiencing the scenery, enjoying a vacation, attending interpretative demonstrations, and visiting facilities and visitor centers that offer information about the parkway.

A significant relationship was also found between the visitors' reasons for visiting the parkway and their preferences for scenery ($\chi^2 = 26.69$, df = 1, P = .001). Tourists liking the open scene, as exemplified in Figure 4.1, were interested in scenery in general and learning about the parkway culture. But they also liked the least preferred unmaintained scenes ($\chi^2 = 7.78$, df = 1, P = .005). Tourists who did not like an open scenic view did not share such sightseeing motives. As a result, management practices might be geared toward the scenic recreational experiences for tourists who like both the open and unmaintained vistas. This shared preference among the tourists certainly helps simplify the manager's decision about the level of maintenance required for scenic overlooks. Although the manager may err in providing an optimal visual experience by keeping an open visual corridor through an overlook to some distant scene, the majority of the tourists will be satisfied since they like both unmaintained and open vistas. The manager could hardly wish for a more cooperative tourist to visit the parkway.

Scenic Preferences of Tourists

Tourists were asked to respond to a wide selection of photos that represented scenes along the Blue Ridge Parkway. In addition to the photos, the tourists were asked a separate set of questions regarding their preferences for the natural vs. man-made elements of a scene (see Appendix A). Factoring and Alpha procedures were used to classify the elements in a scene. Two factors, one relating to natural elements and the other relating to the more rural farm, pastoral, or man-made elements, emerged. Statistical Factor loadings and Alpha scores are reported in Table 4.2.

The Factor scores and Alpha levels were acceptable with regard to the natural and the man-made rural elements of scenery. We tested the relationship between the stated desirability of certain elements in a scene and their effect upon the tourist's choice of an open or unmaintained scene. In evaluating elements of the rural landscape, including the desirability of small towns, communities, farm buildings, and rivers flowing through farms, tourists who preferred developed rural scenes

Table 4.2. Stated preferences for scenes along the Blue Ridge Parkway.

	Factor	
Items	Natural	Rural
Mountain peaks and ridges	.56	
Rolling hills	.65	
Flowering plants	.55	
Valleys	.70	
Tall trees	.62	
Steep dropoff or cliffs	.41	
Small towns or communities		.71
Rivers flowing through farms		.61
Farms and farm buildings		.80
Eigenvalue	3.15	1.16
Alpha value	.75	.76

liked the open vista, while tourists who disliked the rural, pastoral elements did not like the open vista (χ^2 = 12.72, df = 1, P = .001).

The same relationship existed for the unmaintained vista. Tourists who preferred the rural scene liked the unmaintained vista. Those having no interest in viewing the rural development along the Blue Ridge Parkway had little interest in the unmaintained overlook (χ^2 = 3.23, df = 1, P = .07). Tourists appreciating a natural scene also preferred an unmaintained vista, while tourists not appreciating a natural scene did not like the unmaintained vista (χ^2 = 49.05, df = 1, P = .001). The same pattern was true for the open vistas regarding stated preference for a natural scene (χ^2 = 59.46, df = 1, P = .001). Clearly, a pattern of preferences toward landscape elements existed, which separates the dominant tourist groups. The similarity is striking when we look at the tourists' reasons for traveling along the Blue Ridge and their expectations and environmental attitudes.

Tourists who were sightseeing on a vacation found rural community and farm scenes highly appealing. Those who were not sightseeing did not prefer rural scenes (χ^2 = 13.25, df = 1, P = .001). The natural elements in a scene, such as cliffs, valleys, rolling hills, peaks, ridges, tall trees, and flowers, were also found more appealing by tourists who were sightseeing. Conversely, those not interested in sightseeing did not find those elements of a scene very desirable ($X2$ =13.00, df=1, P= .001). Tourists who are sightseeing tend to like the open and unmaintained scenes and appreciate the combined natural and rural themes that are found along the Blue Ridge Parkway. A better script could not be written for a parkway manager, since the sightseeing tourist likes the full range of scenes along the parkway.

Conclusions

If we were to exclude all consideration of attitudes, expectations, and values for visiting the parkway, management would be dealing with a general visiting public (as reported by Hammitt in Chapter 2) that prefers open scenes with views of multi-ridged vistas and expresses a dislike for scenes that obscure the distant views. However, the parkway manager cannot ask the visiting public to leave behind their preferences for scenery, their attitudes toward nature, or their reasons for visiting the parkway. The parkway manager needs to realize that part of the visiting public cares very much for all aspects of the parkway. Tourists generally express consistent positive preferences for landscape and scenery based upon their attitudes, beliefs, or motives. Another tourist segment, which is consistently negative, does not share those beliefs or motives, and the remaining tourist segment is essentially neutral.

The real question facing managers is whether to maintain vistas as open or unmaintained. The choice is quite clear. They can do both and satisfy the visiting public. The results of our analysis, however, lead inevitably to the following questions: What is the optimal ratio of open to unmaintained vistas along the parkway? Should the current ratio be changed or maintained? Should it be a two-to-one, a three-to-one, or a four-to-one ratio of open to unmaintained vistas? That ratio remains an issue. The management challenge is to determine the proper mix to continue providing satisfactory sightseeing experiences for tourists in the most cost-effective way.

REFERENCES

Andrews, Richard. 1979. Landscape values in public decisions. Paper presented at the National Conference on Applied Techniques for Analysis and Management of the Visual Resource, Incline Village, Nevada. pp. 687–688.

Berry, David. 1976. Preservation of open space and the concept of value. *American Journal of Economics and Sociology* 35(2):114–118.

Buhyoff, G. J., J. D. Wellman, H. Harvey, and R. A. Fraser. 1978. Landscape architects' interpretations of people's landscape preferences. *Journal of Environmental Management* 6(3):255–262.

Carls, Glenn. 1974. The effects of people and man-induced conditions on preferences for outdoor recreation landscape. *Journal of Leisure Research* 6 (Spring): 113–114.

Craik, Kenneth. 1975. Individual variations in landscape description. *In* Zube, Brush, and Fabos (eds.) *Landscape Assessment Values, Perceptions, and Resources.* Stroudsburg, PA: Dowden, Hutchinson & Ross.

Dunlap, Riley, and Kent D. Van Liere. 1978. *Environmental Concern.* Illinois: Vance Bibliographics.

Kaplan, Rachel. 1977. Patterns of environmental preference. *Environment and Behavior* 9 (June):195–216.

Kates, Robert. 1966–67. The pursuit of beauty in the environment. *Landscape* 12 (Winter):21–5.

Lowenthal, David. 1962–63. Not every prospect pleases—what is our criterion for beauty? *Landscape* 12 (Winter):19–23.

Mitchell, Arnold. 1983. *American Lifestyles.* New York: MacMillan Publishing.

Moeller, George, Robert MacLachlan, and Douglas Morrison. 1974. Measuring perception of elements in outdoor environments. USDA Paper NE-289, Upper Darby, PA.

Noe, F. P., Gary Hampe, and Linda Malone. 1981. Outdoor recreation sporting patterns' effect on aesthetic evaluation of parkway scenes. *International Journal of Sport Psychology* 12(2):96–104.

Rose, M. A. 1975. Visual quality in land use control. Working Paper No. 1, School of Landscape Architecture, Syracuse, NY: State University of New York.

Shafer, Elwood, John Hamilton, and Elizabeth Schmidt. 1969. Natural landscape preferences: a predictive model. *Journal of Leisure Research* 1 (Winter): 14–15.

Yeosting, D. R., and W. G. Beardsley. 1973. Recreation preferences, use patterns, and value estimation. *In* Larry Whiting (ed.) *Seminar Papers, Land Use Planning Seminar: Focus on Iowa.* Center for Agric. and Rural Development, Iowa St. Univ., Ames.

Zube, Ervin, David Pitt, and Thomas Anderson. 1975. Perception and prediction of scenic resource values of the northeast. *In* Zube, Brush, and Fabos (eds.) *Landscape Assessment: Values, Perceptions, and Resources.* Stroudsburg, PA: Dowden, Hutchinson, and Ross.

Zube, Ervin, James Sell, and Jonathan G. Taylor. 1984. Landscape perception: research, application, and theory. Unpublished manuscript. Univ. of Arizona, Tucson.

Chapter Five
Visual Experiences of Sightseers

J. Douglas Wellman, Gregory J. Buhyoff,
Nick R. Feimer, and Michael R. Patsfall
Virginia Polytechnic Institute and State University
Blacksburg, Virginia

The American public's concern with natural landscape beauty has grown as undeveloped, unblemished landscapes have disappeared. Economic exploitation during our national history has increased the value of the remaining pristine lands. At the same time, however, economic development has supported the arts and humanities, which have taught us to appreciate nature, and has provided the wealth that allows us to preserve national landscapes.

Since at least as early as the 1864 Yosemite Grant, our concern with the beauty of natural landscapes has been recognized in national policy and in the actions of our leading land management agencies. From the beginning, the National Park Service has had scenic preservation as one of its major management objectives. In the U.S. Forest Service, systematic efforts to protect and enhance landscape scenic beauty did not come until the 1970s. Then the clearcutting controversy combined with the environmental movement to produce the Visual Management System (Zube, 1976; Zube et al., 1982).

The new Forest Service effort, like the long-standing Park Service effort, is based on the expert judgments of landscape architects. However, numerous studies have shown that expert views may not reflect those of the interested public. Furthermore, managerial decisions about public resources should take into account the wishes of those members of the public who do not use resources directly but still may be interested in them. More generally, deference to experts has not been one of the hallmarks of public decision-making in the era following the Viet Nam War. The American public has demonstrated its desire to be involved in agency actions that affect it, and this is particularly true in matters pertaining to the environment. The national parks and forests belong to the public, and all citizens should have the opportunity to express their opinions about how they should be managed. However, it is impossible to obtain public opinion on every management decision involving scenic beauty, and to do so with quantitative measures sensitive to small changes in objective environmental conditions.

As a way of incorporating public aesthetic judgments into land management, the psychophysical landscape evaluation approach was developed. The goal of this research is to develop mathematical models that express the relationship between observable landscape features and perceived scenic beauty. If good models can be found, then land managers can estimate in advance the effects that alternative courses of action will have on scenic quality. The intent is not to replace the expert judgments of landscape architects, but to complement them.

This chapter is based on research using the psychophysical approach to scenic beauty assessment. In Part I, we review the steps we have taken over the last decade to develop this approach and apply it to park and forest aesthetic management decision-making. This is a brief nontechnical overview intended to provide a general framework for understanding the research we have done at the Blue Ridge Parkway. Readers wishing greater detail are referred to other publications. In Part II, we present the findings of our work, using this approach, on the Blue Ridge Parkway. It is technical and assumes a working knowledge of statistics.

Part I
Development of Our Approach to Landscape Beauty Assessment

Psychophysics
The first step was to devise a reliable and valid way of measuring scenic beauty. For this we turned to the branch of psychology known as psychophysics. This imposing name reflects the effort, in progress since the latter half of the nineteenth century, to calibrate the relationship between physical phenomena like length, weight, loudness, and brightness, and human responses to them.

The field of psychophysics grew out of German philosophers' attempts to understand how the mind works by comparing observable objects with unobservable psychological responses. This line of inquiry was refined over the years, with major boosts from defense, engineering, and marketing, among other interests. The armed services' interest in the behavior of radar interpreters, for example, led to the development of the Signal Detection Theory (Green and Swetts, 1966), one of the major breakthroughs in psychophysics and the foundation for much of the current work in quantitative landscape assessment. Engineers were concerned with human responses to alternative control and display panel arrays, and their efforts at practical applications have greatly enriched the theory and methodology of psychophysics. Market researchers have employed psychophysical approaches to assess such intangibles as the attractiveness to prospective buyers of alternative automobile styles and the "Italianness" of alternative formulations of spaghetti sauce. In all these applications, psychophysical theory and methods have proven to be useful in decisions involving human life and large amounts of money.

Out of all the work on psychophysics over the years, the most solid product, by wide consensus, is Thurstone's Law of Comparative Judgment (Thurstone, 1927). This is where we began 10 years ago in our efforts to work quantitatively with natural landscape beauty. A brief, non-technical presentation of the theory and our application follows; for a thorough discussion, the reader is referred to Buhyoff and Leuschner (1978), Buhyoff and Riesenman (1979), and Hull et al. (1984).

Law of Comparative Judgment Scaling

The essential idea behind Thurstonian scaling is that people can differentiate among stimuli along some given dimension, but that for any given stimulus people's evaluations will vary somewhat depending on such things as their mood and other stimuli present or in memory. Thus, for any stimulus, repeated evaluations in terms of any particular dimension (e.g., weight, brightness, loudness, beauty, "Italianness," attractiveness for purchase) will be arrayed as a distribution of scores around a mean. The more similar two stimuli are perceived to be, the greater the overlap in their distributions.

While we cannot observe the underlying dimension of interest, we can observe the response distributions for particular stimuli that are presumed to vary in the amount of beauty, loudness, or "Italianness" they contain. By presenting subjects with a set of stimuli that vary along some dimension and by comparing the distributions of their responses to each, we can develop an interval scale of the dimension under study. That interval metric is the key to developing mathematical models relating landscape beauty to physical landscape features. Such models allow us to begin bringing the general public's views into landscape management in ways that are meaningful and useful to park and forest managers.

Our First Application of Thurstonian Scaling: Southern Pine Beetle Damage Along the Blue Ridge Parkway

Perhaps the most effective way to present our use of psychophysical laws in landscape evaluation is to describe some of the research we have done. In the process we will address a number of methodological issues we have encountered and thus expand the discussion of psychophysical scaling as we have applied it.

Our first application was on the Blue Ridge Parkway (Buhyoff and Leuschner, 1978). There was concern at that time with the visual impact of southern pine beetle damage that could be seen from the parkway. Park management was interested in knowing whether the public was aware of and concerned about this damage. They wanted expressions of public response to be in a form that was sensitive enough to minor changes to be useful in guiding decisions about forest protection or salvage.

An issue we confronted immediately was that of response bias. The widely used survey research approaches seemed in this case very susceptible to bias. If we simply asked the visitors whether they noticed and were concerned about pine beetle damage, we felt there was a good chance of obtaining invalid data, as people sought to avoid appearing unaware or unconcerned. The alternative approach of showing people slides and asking them how much they liked the landscapes depicted in them seemed more valid. Furthermore, by informing some subjects about the pine beetle damage while not informing others, we could exercise experimental control over the response bias issue.

The next question concerned how to show the slides. For this we turned to the psychophysics literature and employed the pair comparison method. Ten slides, varying by expert judgment in the extent and stage of pine beetle damage but as similar as possible in all other respects (e.g., forest type, absence of visible traces of man's presence, cloud cover, slope, season, distance from viewer), were selected from several hundred photos taken along the parkway. All possible pairings of these slides were shown to groups of subjects, one pair at a time, and in each case they were asked simply to indicate with a check on a response form whether they preferred the scene shown on the right or the left. By applying Thurstonian scaling to the resultant matrix of proportions—the proportion of times slide A was preferred over slides B, C, etc.—we then arrived at the interval-level preference scores we needed for use as a dependent variable in regression modeling.

Our subjects for this research were not parkway visitors, but college students in several different fields, Sierra Club members, professional foresters, and ordinary citizens. In at least seventeen instances, previous research had demonstrated that people's responses to slides are a valid reflection of their responses to actual landscapes, so we felt justified in using slides. Previous research had also shown that college students' responses were valid representations of the general public's responses. This knowledge permitted us to employ readily available college student populations in our research, thereby avoiding unnecessary interruption of parkway visits, saving time and scarce research funds, and improving control over viewing conditions.

While relying on college students alone would have been defensible, we went to groups of the general public, Sierra Club members, and Weyerhaeuser Corporation foresters to confirm the validity of college student responses. We found no difference in the responses of these groups, which we assumed represented a full range of orientation toward nature. Therefore, we concluded that our research approach was free from the response bias that concerned us.

With our dependent variable data thus in hand, the next stage was to establish the relationship between these psychophysical data and physical landscape features. For this we used regression modelling. For this modelling, we needed predictor variables that were reliable, sensitive, and potentially useful to managers. Through a grid analysis procedure for each slide, we measured the proportion of vegetated area with visible pine beetle damage. We then carried out regression analysis to determine the relationship between the physically observable damage measure and the unobservable psychophysical preference measure. Given the controlled character of the slide set we used, the single variable of proportion of vegetative area showing pine beetle damage was a highly significant predictor. It accounted for 33% of the variance in the responses of the uninformed subjects and 84% of the variance for the informed subjects. For both groups of subjects, the shape of the regression curves was similar. Visual preference dropped very rapidly with increasing beetle damage until approximately the 10% level, after which point there were much smaller psychophysical impacts. Our practical recommendation to managers was that they concentrate their pest control efforts on preventing initial outbreaks since once damage had become visible, its extent did not matter greatly. In making this recommendation, we also recognized that a multiplicity of other concerns might shape managerial response to pine beetle outbreaks. Several years later we replicated our findings with different subjects, thus increasing our confidence in the general approach and our previous findings (Buhyoff et al., 1980).

At about the time of the southern pine beetle study, we learned several other items of interest to the general field of psychophysical landscape preference research. The first relates to the validity of using respondent panels to represent public preferences. In a related study, also based on slides from the Blue Ridge Parkway (Harvey, 1977), one of our panels consisted of college students majoring in art. We found that their preferences differed from those of the other students we studied. Whether from selection or training, design-oriented students evidently employed a different set of criteria in evaluating landscapes. If design professionals look at landscapes differently from the general public, the question arises as to how accurately landscape architects can define and respond to public preferences. This is of obvious importance in such expert-oriented planning as that employed by the Park Service and Forest Service.

In another related study, we asked a panel of landscape architects to evaluate a set of slides as they felt our student panels would. We then asked the landscape architects to read statements the students had written about what they generally liked and did not like about the slides. Finally, we asked the landscape architects once again to predict student evaluation of the slides. The landscape architects' initial predictions were significantly off the mark, but after they had read the statements their predictions were generally accurate (Buhyoff et al., 1978). This finding demonstrates the value of conditioning expert-oriented landscape evaluation systems with information on public preferences.

The second methodological issue we explored concerned potential bias resulting from mixing the seasons that slides depict and in which they are shown. In this research (Buhyoff and Wellman, 1979) we demonstrated that the same set of slides could receive differing evaluations, depending on the season in which they were rated. Slides that appeared to show fall coloration (actually the red stage of southern pine beetle damage) were given relatively high preference scores at the end of the summer before any true fall color changes had occurred and relatively low preference ratings during the winter months before spring greening had occurred. We attributed this to what we called an "anticipation bias," which is probably a form of novelty effect.

The third methodological exploration pursued in the southern pine beetle study concerned the functional form of the preference curves derived from the regression analyses. A logarithmic function best described the scatter of observations relating the areal extent of pine beetle damage to viewer preferences. The literature of psychophysics and our own data sets suggested that in future research the *a priori* specification of non-linear functions was appropriate, and in our subsequent research we have done so (Buhyoff and Wellman, 1980).

Adoption of Scenic Beauty Estimation Approach: Aesthetic Impacts of Forest Pest Infestations in Colorado

At the time we were developing our approach to quantitative landscape evaluation, a related research initiative was being pursued under the leadership of Terry Daniel of the University of Arizona. The aforementioned Signal Detection Theory, a psychophysical approach conceptually related to the Law of Comparative Judgment, served as the foundation of this landscape assessment approach (Daniel and Boster, 1976). Called the Scenic Beauty Estimation method, this new approach permitted the use of far more landscape slides. This was attractive, since viewer fatigue becomes a major concern after about a dozen slides in the pair-comparison method. It is obviously difficult to adequately represent all the landscape conditions of interest in so few slides.

An opportunity to compare our approach with Daniel's was provided by the U.S. Forest Service's Forest Insect and Disease Management program, which sought a multidisciplinary evaluation of the mountain pine beetle and western spruce budworm infestations in the front range of the Colorado Rockies. Terry Daniel was the leader of the in-stand aesthetic modeling, and we carried out the work on scenic vistas.

The in-stand modeling approach consisted of randomly selecting points within the forest, photographing what was seen from those points, and then inventorying the area using standard forestry procedures. Measures taken included such parameters as the size and species of the trees, presence and amount of down wood and understory vegetation, and evidence of insect damage. Panels of students and other representatives of the public were shown the slides, and an interval preference scale was developed using Scenic Beauty Estimation procedures.

The forest inventory data were then regressed on the visual preference scores to develop predictive models of the impacts of insect damage on scenic beauty, taking into account other characteristics of the forest. This approach has the great advantage of linking public perceptions of scenic beauty directly with an ongoing forest inventory, so that data-based planning systems, which integrate aesthetic concerns with other forest management objectives, can be used.

For the Colorado study, we used an approach similar to that used in the southern pine beetle study on the Blue Ridge Parkway. The first major difference concerned the slide sets. In the Rockies the slides used were far less controlled. Whereas in the parkway study variation between slides was limited almost completely to the amount of visible insect damage, the Colorado slide set included a wide array of other variables. This difference in the slide sets was due both to differences in the nature of the landscapes, with visibility in the western study being far greater and therefore including many more elements, and to the nature of the research design. By adopting the Scenic Beauty Estimation procedure, we were able to use much larger slide sets and thus incorporate a far broader array of landscape elements. Additionally, while in the southern pine beetle study we sought to examine a "worst-case" condition, wherein visitor attention would be strongly drawn to the insect damage, in the Colorado study our goal was to assess the visual impact of the pest infestations within the context of the overall landscape, including snow-capped mountains seen at a great distance, intermediate-distance rock formations, forest vegetation, and other natural features. As before, we attempted to exclude man-made landscape features as much as possible.

The second major difference between the two studies came in our use of the Scenic Beauty Estimation procedure for developing the dependent variable measure. In this procedure, panels of subjects evaluate slide sets so that any given slide is seen only once. Since there is no repetition of the pair-comparison method, viewer fatigue is generally far less of a problem. However, since the Law of Comparative Judgment is the touchstone theory and the pair-comparison method the most carefully tested measurement approach in psychophysics, we did not want to relax constraints on stimuli at the cost of measurement quality. Therefore, we carried out Law of Comparative Judgment scaling on a subsample of the Scenic Beauty Estimation slide set (Hull et al., 1984). Our results indicated no significant differences in the quality of the resulting metrics, and we have therefore employed the Scenic Beauty Estimation method in all our subsequent research.

Methodologically, then, the mountain pine beetle-western spruce budworm study was an important step. Substantive findings were of interest as well in comparison with our Blue Ridge Parkway findings. As noted above, the parkway slides contained little variation other than pest damage and thus represented a "worst case" condition. The Colorado vistas, on the other hand, included a great deal of landscape variation in addition to pest damage.

In our multiple regression analysis of the Colorado slides, we found that visible pest damage entered the equation not only with the anticipated negative weighting, but also with limited overall predictive power (pest damage was important for informed observers, but not for uninformed observers). Generally speaking, the rich and often striking landscape elements in the Colorado slides overwhelmed the effects of pest damage. We recommended that priority in visual management be given to those areas where visible pest damage was relatively close to the visitor and not surrounded by extensive views or spectacular landforms (Buhyoff et al., 1982).

A second substantive finding of interest was the relationship between the area of sharp mountains in a scene and scenic beauty. We found that scenic beauty increased with increasing area of sharp mountains up to a moderate point, after which scenic beauty dropped as the area in sharp mountains continued to increase. This finding raised the question of whether such a relationship holds for other landscape elements.

In our first urban forestry project, reported below, we found evidence that scenic preference rose with increasing tree size (and leaf presence) up to a point, after which it declined. We had insufficient data in that study to draw any firm conclusions, but combined with our results on sharp mountains from Colorado, the urban data led us to the tentative hypothesis that "too much of a good thing" may best describe extreme conditions in landscapes.

In-Stand Modeling: The Urban Forestry and Private Landowners Projects

In addition to adopting Daniel's Scenic Beauty Estimation Method, we have in several projects worked with his in-stand modeling procedure. The objective of this procedure is to develop predictive equations expressing the relationship between scenic beauty and standard forest inventory measures. Previous in-stand modeling work had focused on the relatively open forest of the West, in Colorado and Arizona. Our uses of the in-stand approach were in the densely foliated Eastern forest and in urban settings.

In the urban study (Buhyoff et al., 1984), our goal was to quantitatively identify those characteristics of the urban forest most strongly related to perceived scenic beauty and to do so in terms meaningful to urban forest managers. We photographed street scenes in Ann Arbor and Dearborn, Michigan, had student panels at the University of Michigan and Virginia Polytechnic Institute scale the scenic beauty of the slides, and developed models of scenic beauty for both our own forest inventory data and for data from the regular inventory of the forest manager in Ann Arbor. Practical management questions, such as the importance of species diversity and the value of maintaining large, old trees were among the concerns behind the project.

We found that species diversity had a small, positive relationship with scenic beauty, while tree size had a larger positive relationship. Methodologically, we were most interested in the aesthetic information that might be embedded in the ongoing forest inventory. We wanted to know whether scenic beauty could be estimated solely on the basis of the inventory and with sufficient precision to guide management decisions. Our findings in the first study were very encouraging, and a follow-up study has shown that urban forest inventory data bases can be used to predict scenic beauty. For a larger sample of sites, using only the Ann Arbor forest inventory data, we developed regression equations that explained 58% of the variation in scenic beauty evaluations (Lien et al., 1984).

The last study to be reviewed here focused on the long-standing forestry issue of how to encourage scientific management of nonindustrial private forests (Vodak et al., 1985). Our specific purpose was to determine how landowner assessments of forest scenic beauty were related to actual forest conditions, since beliefs about the aesthetic consequences of forest management may deter landowners from acting as foresters would like them to act. Our landscape assessment procedure is, we believe, relatively free of the potential semantic bias problems faced by researchers using survey techniques to obtain opinions on forest management techniques. In addition, we could design the experiment to assess potential bias in the same way we had done in the southern pine beetle study.

We selected stands on the Jefferson National Forest (predominantly the oak-hickory forest type characteristic of the mountainous areas of the Southern Appalachian region) where we knew the management history. Stands were pre-stratified according to whether they had been clearcut, heavily thinned, lightly thinned, or not managed. At randomly selected points within each stand, we took photographs and carried out a standard forest inventory. We then had the slides evaluated for scenic beauty by landowner and student panels, and we conducted model-building regression analyses.

Our models demonstrated that clearcut and heavily thinned stands were less preferred than lightly thinned and unmanaged areas, and that the presence of dead and down wood was the strongest predictor of negative scenic beauty ratings. Our major practical recommendation from this study was that slash reduction and removal be required in cases where appearance is a concern. Methodologically, the study was a significant extension of Daniel's work on the ponderosa pine forest type of the western United States to a very different forest type. In addition, by informing some respondent panels about the management history of the scenes and comparing their answers to uninformed subjects, we demonstrated that semantic bias may not be a serious concern in research on forest management preferences.

Conclusions, Part I

Behind the Blue Ridge Parkway study reported next, then, are numerous studies conducted over nearly a decade's time and supported by the work of other researchers. We have presented the main line in the development of our program, but there were many other inquiries as well, including studies related to alternative ways of scaling scenic beauty (Buhyoff et al., 1981), alternative modeling approaches (Propst and Buhyoff 1981), and the projection of scenic beauty to future forest conditions (Hull, 1984). We have also restricted our review of others' work to the quantitative modeling work of Terry Daniel and his colleagues. Many others have contributed to the quantitative approach. Finally, we have not touched on the major alternative approach to landscape beauty assessment, the transactional approach, which predicts scenic beauty from relatively abstract, non-physical variables such as complexity and coherence.

Part II
Scenic Beauty and Vegetation Management on Blue Ridge Parkway Vistas

In what follows we will present in detail our research on the aesthetic aspects of vegetation management on Blue Ridge Parkway vistas. Our specific purpose in this research was to describe quantitatively how public perceptions of vista scenic beauty are affected by foreground vegetation. In previous research, foreground vegetation had frequently been shown to have a negative relation to scenic beauty. Therefore, vegetation management is a potentially important element of any overall effort to provide quality experiences for parkway visitors. In addition, manipulation of foreground vegetation is one of the few management actions that may be practical to maintain and enhance scenic vistas. Yet foreground vegetation management at vistas is neither cost-free nor wholly non-controversial (e.g., controversy about herbicide use), so research clarifying its aesthetic consequences is desirable.

The Distance Class Variable in Physicalistic Landscape Preference Research

Studies using physicalistic variables as predictors of visual aesthetic landscape quality have commonly included a set of distance classes for vegetation. A tripartite division of distance classes is most common, with visible vegetation classified as being in the foreground, middleground, or background of the scene based upon general criteria of visual resolution. However, efforts to test the utility of such delineations of vegetation distance have met with mixed success. For example, Shafer et al. (1969) found that the areal perimeter of immediate (i.e., foreground) vegetation in the landscape photos was a significant predictor of preference for the scenes. They also reported a number of significant higher order terms involving foreground vegetation, including: the perimeter of immediate vegetation; the perimeter of immediate vegetation multiplied by the perimeter of distant vegetation; the perimeter of immediate vegetation multiplied by the area of intermediate (i.e., middleground) vegetation; and the perimeter of immediate vegetation squared.

Brush and Palmer (1979) found that the use of distance classes increased prediction of scenic quality by 10% over sum total indices. On the other hand, Arthur (1977) included the presence of foreground, middleground, and background (measured on a five-point rating scale from "presence of foreground only" to "presence of all distance classes") and found it failed to predict an index of perceived scenic beauty of Arizona forest landscapes. Similarly, Propst and Buhyoff (1980), employing a regression procedure known as policy capturing, found foreground vegetation to be a relatively inconsequential predictor of landscape preferences.

Adding to the uncertainty surrounding the role of vegetation distance classes is Weinstein's (1976) caveat concerning the application of multivariate statistical procedures in studies such as the one reported by Shafer et al. (1969). He points out that environment-behavior researchers are at times unduly insensitive to problems of model overfitting, which result from chance variation in the data set or loss of degrees of freedom. As a result, one can expect the generalizability of such studies to be limited.

Another question of interest with respect to vegetation distance is whether or not the particular placement of these landscape elements in the image field has any impact on perceived scenic beauty. That is to say, does it matter if the background imagery is in the left, center, or right portion of the image? Traditional notions about aesthetic composition would suggest that it might. For example, one frequently used convention of aesthetic composition is to have the elements of primary importance centrally placed and surrounded by secondary elements.

Methods

Stimuli. The stimuli consisted of a sample of 63 vista scenes selected from a larger set of 298 photo-slides sampled along the entire length of the Blue Ridge Parkway in the states of Virginia and North Carolina. The total number of scenes selected for the study was to be fewer than 100 to avoid viewer fatigue during the rating procedure. Scenes were evaluated for inclusion in the sample according to three criteria: (1) representativeness, (2) the quality of scenic characteristics, and (3) photographic quality. Sites were also chosen not to be extreme in terms of the quality of their scenic characteristics. That is, the scenes should not have been atypically high or low in scenic quality. These selection criteria were used to ensure that the models developed were applicable to conditions most generally found along the parkway. However, few scenes were excluded on that basis.

The vistas were photographed from positions and perspectives that were as nearly equivalent as possible and under relatively similar atmospheric conditions (i.e., under generally clear skies with only minor haze and cloud cover). Scenes that were excessively cloudy were rephotographed at a later time. Finally, the photographs selected for use in the study had to be of good photographic quality. Slide selection and elimination were by consensus of three of the investigators.

Scaling of Scenic Beauty. Forty-one introductory psychology students at Virginia Polytechnic Institute and State University rated each of the 63 scenes on a 10-point scale (one was "low," 10 was "high"). The subjects were instructed to rate each scene according to its "scenic beauty," defined simply as "the overall scenic quality of the landscape, its general beauty." Each 35-mm color transparency was projected for eight seconds, with a period of eight seconds between each slide in which the screen was blank but lighted. The scenes were presented in random order. The Scenic Beauty Estimation (SBE) method (Daniel and Boster, 1976) was used to derive an interval scale of scenic beauty from the scenic beauty ratings. This method employs Thurstonian scaling procedures (Guilford, 1954; Torgerson, 1958) and signal detection theory (Green and Swetts, 1966) to transform the rating distributions of a group of individuals into an interval scale of perceived beauty. The Scenic Beauty Estimate (SBE) produced for each scene is the dm value (multiplied by 100) in signal detection theory.

Scene Feature Analysis. For each photograph, physical features were measured by digitizing landscape elements from outlines projected on $8'' \times 11''$ paper. The digitizing process uses a computer-connected stylus that, among other things, produces areal measures from tracing over any two-dimensional figure or outline. Foreground, middleground, and background were delineated for each photograph. Foreground consisted of that area of the photograph for which individual leaves of the vegetation were discernible. Middleground was that portion of the scene for which forms, or outlines, of trees and other vegetation were distinguishable but lacking fine detail. Background was that area of the photo for which the crown shapes of individual trees were not distinguishable.

For the purpose of examining the importance of compositional qualities, each outline was also divided vertically into equal left, center, and right sections. The area in each photo of foreground vegetation (FV), middleground vegetation (MV), and background vegetation (BV) was digitized for each section. This horizontal and vertical division resulted in nine such variables: left foreground vegetation (LFV), center foreground vegetation (CFV), and so on (see Table 5.1 for the complete list of variables). All variables were recorded in units of square inches.

We also recorded the total area of cloud cover (TCL), the number of discrete clouds (NC), dichotomous measures of the presence of man-made impacts (MI), the presence of haze (H), the presence of clouds (CL), and the geographic section (indicating north/south location) of the parkway from which the scene was sampled (AREA). The human impacts were generally views of residential and commercial areas in the far middleground or background, were small in scale relative to the entire scene, and revealed little detail. Because the focus of the study was principally directed at delineating the effects of vegetation, clouds and human impacts were not measured with regard to lateral placement in the scene.

The AREA variable was included to provide an indicator of the effects of general topographic and vegetative features, which might not be fully represented by the digitized variables. The AREA variable was created by dividing the parkway into five sections of approximately 95 miles each (running from north to south) and assigning numbers from one to five (beginning with one for the northernmost section) to each section of the parkway from which each scene was taken.

The distance from one end of the parkway to the other represents an ecosystem gradient that varies with respect to topography and vegetation. The terrain at the northern end of the parkway is relatively low in altitude and flat in surface variation, with altitude and "ruggedness" (or surface variation) increasing as one moves south. Vegetation at the northern end of the parkway is primarily deciduous, with a gradual and continual increase in coniferous vegetation when one moves south.

Results and Discussion

The reliability of the SBE ratings was computed using the method delineated by Ebel (1981). Using the mean squares produced from an analysis of variance where scenes are a random independent variable, both the average inter-judge agreement (correlation) and the composite reliability of the group of judges may be ascertained. The former represents the reliability of a single rater, and the latter the reliability of the summed or averaged vector of ratings for the same number of judges used in the analysis. In this instance, the intraclass correlation is 0.23 and the composite reliability is 0.92. Thus, the average degree of agreement among individual subjects is relatively low, but the reliability of the composite scores for scenes, which were used for subsequent analysis, is quite high. This latter measure of reliability is much more relevant to the current study than is the former, since the purpose of the study is to predict the general pattern of responses in a rather diverse population.

Because the measurement of these image properties was conducted by a single researcher, a direct appraisal of the reliability of the independent variables was not possible. Because of the substantial time and expense involved in the measurement of these variables, their duplication for a large enough sample of scenes to derive a reasonable estimate of reliability is normally not feasible. However, the criteria for the delineation of distance classes and the measurement of image features are highly circumscribed, requiring little subjective judgment. The reliability of such measures has generally been regarded to be extremely high and is rarely appraised or reported.

Descriptive statistics for all variables are presented in Table 5.1, and zero-order intercorrelations among them in Table 5.2. Regression models were formulated using a best subset procedure.

Table 5.1. Summary of descriptive statistics for model.

Variable Definitions[1]	Mean	SD
BV = Total area of background vegetation	8.92	5.34
FV = Total area of foreground vegetation	26.97	14.22
MV = Total area of middleground vegetation	13.26	9.90
LBV = Area of background vegetation in left section	2.72	2.20
CBV = Area of background vegetation in center section	3.62	2.11
RBV = Area of background vegetation in right section	2.57	1.87
LFV = Area of foreground vegetation in left section	10.10	5.89
CFV = Area of foreground vegetation in center section	7.48	3.99
RFV = Area of foreground vegetation in right section	9.39	5.34
LMV = Area of middleground vegetation in left section	3.80	3.27
CMV = Area of middleground vegetation in center section	4.95	3.79
RMV = Area of middleground vegetation in right section	4.50	3.96
NC = Number of discrete clouds	2.05	1.70
TCL = Total area covered by clouds	15.84	11.89
SBE1 = Scenic Beauty Estimate of Scenes in Study 1	0.00	45.00
SBE2 = Scenic Beauty Estimate of Scenes in Study 2	0.00	31.92
Categorical Variables	Frequency	
CL = Presence of clouds	59	
H = Presence of haze	33	
MI = Presence of human impacts	29	
AREA = Section of the parkway where scene was sampled		
1	18	
2	5	
3	8	
4	16	
5	16	

[1]Area is in square inches.

Initially, all possible combinations of up to six predictors were constituted. No more than six predictors were examined in any one model to insure no greater than a 10% ratio of predictors to observations (i.e., to avoid overfitting the data). Since the analyses were for exploratory as well as predictive purposes, a family of models was examined rather than searching for a particular model. The family of models was initially chosen on the basis of the highest R square. Subsequently, models were compared with regard to their F ratios, PRESS statistics, coefficient signficance, and variance inflation factors (Draper and Smith, 1981; Montgomery and Peck, 1982).

The best models for the sectioned (left, center, and right vegetation) variables are presented in Table 5.3, and the best models for the unsectioned (total area) variables are presented in Table 5.4. The sectioned and unsectioned variables were analyzed separately, since the latter are a linear combination of the former.

Table 5.2. Correlations among predictor and criterion variables for model.

	BV	RV	LFV	CFV	RFV	LMV	CMV	RMV	LBV	CBV	RBV	TCL	NC	SBE1	SBE2	AREA
FV	-.820	-.567	.928	.921	.949	-.733	-.716	-.759	-.640	-.274	-.555	-.071	.254	-.388	-.110	.023
MV		.302	-.688	-.853	-.787	.837	.943	.907	.378	.079	.328	-.103	.124	.469	.228	-.063
BV			-.573	-.512	-.494	.319	.211	.290	.883	.845	.864	-.002	.114	.260	.046	.119
LFV				.763	.798	-.768	-.536	-.573	-.654	-.307	-.523	-.075	-.265	-.443	-.166	.079
CFV					.865	-.676	-.841	-.771	-.571	-.260	-.498	-.049	-.239	-.400	-.166	.011
RFV						-.601	-.686	-.814	-.557	-.198	-.531	-.070	-.204	-.245	.103	-.304
LMV							.708	.588	.324	.142	.370	-.134	.211	.518	.285	-.142
CMV								.816	.294	-.024	.283	-.124	.127	.424	.213	-.094
RMV									.397	.105	.243	-.028	.014	.340	.131	.048
LBV										.589	.680	.045	.067	.190	.000	.095
CBV											.592	.038	.094	.312	.189	.099
RBV												-.013	.140	.166	.082	.116
TCL													-.151	-.085	-.154	.159
NCL														.365	.307	-.624
SBE1															.827	-.361
SBE2																-.403

n = 63

r = .248 Significant at p = .05

Table 5.3. Best regression models for sectioned variables.

Model	R^2	Overall F	PRESS	Variable	Standardized Coefficient	P > |t|	Variance Inflation Factor
1	.55	11.28 (p < .0001)	69075.81	Left Foreground (LFV)	-.627	.0005	3.54
				Right Foreground (RFV)	.510	.006	3.96
				Center Middleground (CMV)	.524	.0001	2.03
				Left Background (LBV)	-.333	.024	2.06
				Center Background (CBV)	.456	.002	1.64
				AREA	-.258	.008	1.09
2	.55	10.22 (p < .0001)	73483.62	Left Foreground (LFV)	-.504	.003	3.09
				Right Foreground (RFV)	.486	.012	4.18
				Center Middleground (CMV)	.530	.0002	2.03
				Left Background (LBV)	.414	.001	1.70
				Right Background (RBV)	-.202	.141	2.14
				AREA	-.272	.0065	1.08
3	.54	10.73 (p < .001)	71473.423	Left Foreground (LFV)	-.754	.001	3.66
				Right Foreground (RFV)	.739	.0015	5.91
				Right Middleground (RMV)	.619	.0003	3.13
				Left Background (LBV)	-.338	.023	2.56
				Center Background (CBV)	.393	.0012	1.60
				AREA	-.313	.0016	1.07
4	.53	10.38 (p < .0001)	74571.08	Left Foreground (LFV)	-.555	.0016	3.29
				Right Foreground (RFV)	.768	.0011	5.87
				Center Middleground (CMV)	.351	.0425	3.39
				Right Middleground (RMV)	.345	.1058	5.21
				Center Background (CBV)	.297	.0047	1.20
				AREA	-.304	.0025	1.09

Table 5.4. Best regression models for unsectioned variables.

Model	R²	Overall F	PRESS	Variable	Standardized Coefficient	P > |t|	Variance Inflation Factor
1	.39	5.99 (p < .0001)	96734.06	Foreground (FV)	.244	.288	4.76
				Middleground (MV)	.613	.004	3.82
				Background (BV)	.284	.044	1.76
				Human Impact (MI)	-1.25	.367	1.73
				Haze (H)	-.091	.441	1.26
				AREA	-4.04	.004	1.71
2	.39	5.92 (p < .0001)	98180.40	Foreground (FV)	.274	.256	5.25
				Middleground (MV)	.615	.004	3.98
				Background (BV)	.310	.034	1.86
				Area of Clouds (TCL)	.089	.450	1.25
				Haze (H)	-1.40	.244	1.28
				AREA	.339	.003	1.13
3	.39	5.88 (p < .0001)	96433.02	Foreground (FV)	.284	.243	5.29
				Middleground (MV)	.633	.003	4.03
				Background (BV)	.278	.050	1.77
				Human Impact (MI)	-.135	.330	1.73
				Presence of Clouds (CL)	.051	.660	1.21
				AREA	-.430	.001	1.56
4	.38	5.84 (p < .0001)	97327.98	Foreground (FV)	.266	.272	5.23
				Middleground (MV)	.623	.004	4.09
				Background (BV)	.273	.055	1.77
				Area of Clouds (TCL)	.025	.826	1.22
				Human Impact (MI)	-1.42	.305	1.72
				AREA	-.443	.001	1.49

In general, it appears that breaking down the scenes and using measurements from left, center, and right sections improved the predictive power of the models. The R-square value from the best six-predictor unsectioned model was 0.39 (p <.0001), while for the best six-predictor section model the R-square was 0.5 (p <.0001). Among the findings for the sectioned models, it is interesting to note that LFV and RFV consistently appear as significant predictors of scenic beauty. Foreground vegetation might have been considered irrelevant to the perceived quality of scenic vistas or overlooks unless it simply blocked the vista, but this was not the case. In addition, the regression models for the sectioned variable (see Table 5.3) suggest that there does seem to be a preferred composition. Middle and background vegetation are preferred in the center, and foreground vegetation has an impact on the sides. It should be noted, however, that total foreground vegetation was not a significant predictor of scenic beauty. An examination of the signs of the regression weights for RFV and LFV suggests an explanation for this finding; RFV has a positive weight while LFV has a negative one, indicating that they nullified each other with regard to the overall effect of foreground vegetation on scenic beauty.

The stability of the signs of the regression weights for LFV and RFV was assessed by recalculating models with those two variables eight times while substituting other variables into the model with RFV and LFV. The regression weight signs and their significance were stable across all trials. Thus, the signs of the coefficients for RFV and LFV were not spurious functions of other variables present in the models. However, it is also conceivable that the countervailing signs of LFV and RFV are a result of a suppressor relationship between these two variables. An examination of the correlation matrix (see Table 5.2) does, in fact, suggest such a possibility. In this case both right and left foreground vegetation are negatively correlated with scenic beauty while being positively correlated with one another.

In addition, the zero order correlation between RFV and SBE is not significant (p >0.05). Thus, the change in the RFV regression sign could indicate that LFV and RFV are mutually inhibiting nonpredictive variances. If this is indeed the case, and not a function of other variables, then the relationship should emerge even when no other variables are present in the regression equation. To test this hypothesis, SBE was regressed on LFV and RFV alone. The results of this computation are equivocal but do indicate that any suppression effect between these two predictors is relatively weak. The regression weight signs are the same as in the other equations (standardized coefficients are -0.68 and 0.30 for LFV and RFV, respectively), but the significance test on the RFV regression weight is not significant (p >0.05).

Further supporting the assertion that any suppressor effects are weak are the multicollinearity diagnostics reported in Table 5.3. The variance inflation factors in all models are well below prescribed standards (see Belsley et al., 1980; Montgomery and Peck, 1982), indicating that multicollinearity, of which suppression is a special case, is not problematic.

It also seemed possible that the differences in signs of the regression weights for RFV and LFV could reflect differences in the distribution of amount of foreground vegetation between the left and right sections in the landscape scenes. Inspection of the means (10.10 and 9.39) and standard deviations (5.89 and 5.33) for LFV and RFV, respectively, suggests that this was not the case.

It is conceivable that right and left foreground vegetation differed in ways not adequately assessed by the measures used in this study. For example, it is possible that the type of vegetation (e.g., coniferous versus deciduous) is not evenly dispersed over right and left foreground. The landscape scenes were visually inspected for obvious content differences (i.e., factors such as shape or form, or the presence of coniferous versus deciduous vegetation) once by two of the co-authors and once independently by a third co-author. However, no apparent differences were detected simply by visual inspection.

As noted in Part I of this chapter, previous research (Buhyoff et al., 1982) has suggested a nonmonotonic relationship between perceived scenic beauty and the area of sharp mountains in a scene. The reason for this is unclear. One possibility may be that the greater the area taken up by background, the farther those elements are from the viewer. Consequently, they may lose positive visual qualities associated with scenic beauty, such as detail and texture. In the present study it was hypothesized that such a nonmonotonic relationship might represent the pattern of covariation between total background vegetation and scenic beauty as well. Visual inspection of the plot of residual SBE values versus total background area suggested that such a curvilinearity might be present. To test this, a regression analysis was done on one of the sets of total variables, including total background area (BV), while adding a total background area squared (BV^2) term to the model to test the quadratic effect. Both BV and BV^2 were significant predictors of scenic beauty (standardized $b = 1.21$, $p < .0003$ and $b = -1.07$, $p < .0007$, respectively), suggesting that both linear and nonmonotonic, nonlinear relationships are present in the data.

The findings of the experiment suggest that landscape elements that are general with regard to their content (e.g., amount of background vegetation) are significant predictors of perceived scenic beauty. In addition, the spatial arrangement of these elements was a factor in the prediction of scenic beauty. However, other variables, including various measures of clouds and the presence of haze and human impact, were not predictive. The lack of relationship between these latter variables and perceived scenic beauty may be a function of restriction of range (i.e, extreme values on the continuum were not represented in this sample) or lack of measurement sensitivity. For example, in our sample of scenes, human impact tended to be in the background and was not predominant in the scene. In contrast, prior research has revealed significant effects when human artifacts are primary elements in the scene (Kaplan et al., 1972).

To better understand the nature of the differential weighting of left and right foreground in the prediction of perceived scenic beauty, a second experiment was conducted. The question addressed by this second experiment was whether differential preference for the left and right foreground of the image was a function of image content or was due to a perceptual bias resulting from hemispheric brain specialization (Gazzaniga, 1970; Harcum, 1978). A clear consensus among psychologists concerning the left-right bias has not been reached (Harcum 1978; Heron, 1957; Wickelgren, 1967; Gazzaniga, 1970; Gur et al., 1975).

In the present study, if such a right-left bias persists in monochotic presentations, it is conceivable that differential perception might result. Furthermore, since the majority of the population can be characterized by left side brain specialization (perceptual right side emphasis), right side preference might emerge in a random sample drawn from the population. This bias can be tested by simply reversing the image of the landscape (i.e., by turning the slide around) so that the content on the right side would now appear on the left, and vice versa. If the opposing regression weights are due to the specific content of the image, the new regression weight signs should be opposite to those in study 1. That is, LFV should change from negative to positive, and RFV should shift from positive to negative. If, on the other hand, the opposing regression weights are due to perceptual bias, such as differential processing of information from the left and right fields of vision, it would be expected that the regression weight signs for left and right foreground would remain stable.

In a separate experiment, 39 introductory psychology students at Virginia Polytechnic Institute and State University rated the reversed slides. None of these students had participated in the first study. SBE's were calculated and analyzed as before. The prediction models developed in this study were less successful than in the first one, with average R-square values of 0.36 as compared to 0.53 in the original models. The hypothesized left-right perceptual bias was not found. When the slides were reversed, preferences tended to be reversed as well. Thus, preference appears to be related to content rather than placement of foreground vegetation. In addition, the correlation between the SBE's from the original and the second study was only 0.83 (p <

.0001), somewhat lower than expected on the basis of previous research, and background vegetation was not a significant predictor of scenic quality.

Conclusions and Recommendations

The present findings support previous work (Shafer et al., 1969; Brush and Palmer, 1979) which demonstrated the ability of general content classes of vegetation to predict scenic beauty. Of particular interest is the finding that foreground vegetation can have a substantial impact on the perceived scenic beauty of vistas. Unfortunately, the nature of this impact is complex, as indicated by both the differential regression weights found for LFV and RFV and the lack of impact of total foreground vegetation. There was no support for the notion that a perceptual left-right bias was responsible for the differential weights of LFV and RFV.

The stability of the weights for foreground vegetation suggests that particular foreground content and its placement within a scene are significant predictors of scenic quality. It is puzzling that, while viewers perceive specific content (i.e., left and right foreground) positively or negatively no matter what side of the image it is on, the correlation between SBE's for the original and reversed scenes was only 0.83. This suggests that the perceived quality of the original and reversed scenes is similar but far from identical.

Until the basis for the differential effects of LFV and RFV is better understood, it is difficult to make specific recommendations for management actions. It would obviously be unwise to generalize from the weights found here for left and right foreground to suggest left foreground be inhibited and right foreground be enhanced for any particular scenic overlook. In addition, as Weinstein (1976) has noted, the generalizability of any prediction model must be established by demonstrating its accuracy in other contexts. Thus, the efficacy and utility of these predictors must be evaluated for other sets of landscape scenes and other samples of observers.

The regression models examined in the present study explained a respectable but moderate amount of criterion variance. Nonetheless, a considerable amount of variance in the SBE's went unaccounted for. Given that the findings regarding LFV and RFV remain enigmatic, it may be that other relevant variables or attributes of the scenes went unrecognized, and that these variables may have been able to account for more of the SBE variance. That is, the variables used in these studies (e.g., LFV and RFV) may have been surrogates for these other, unrecognized variables.

The nature of these "other" variables remains unclear, but more complex formulations of environmental attributes must be considered as one variable alternative. Relatively abstract transactional constructs such as complexity, congruity, and mystery have been used effectively in research on environmental aesthetics (Wohlwill, 1968, 1976; Kaplan et al., 1972; Kaplan, 1973, 1975; Wohlwill and Harris, 1980; Feimer et al., 1981; Feimer, 1983), suggesting that a more holistic characterization of the relationships among the elements within the scene may add to prediction beyond that achieved in a simple and gross representation of content.

On a similar but somewhat less abstract plane, it is also conceivable that a more discriminating analysis of content, including an examination of vegetation type and visually salient physical attributes such as shape, form, and color, might add to predictive power. In any case, examination of these other classes of variables in conjunction with the kinds of variables used in this study holds promise for providing insight into the complex pattern of relationships that characterize aesthetic responses to natural settings.

Beyond demonstrating to managers and landscape architects that foreground does matter to visitors, we would like to offer several other observations based on our broader research program.

This research has focused on the foreground vegetation extant at parkway vistas. We have not studied the visual impacts of vegetation manipulation. For example, if controlled burns are used to eradicate unwanted woody plants, there may well be a severe, if temporary, reduction in overall scenic beauty. If mechanical means are used to reduce brushy vegetation, it is advisable to remove the cuttings since all research has demonstrated negative visual impacts from dead and down wood. Obviously, these suggestions must be interpreted in terms of other criteria, in addition to scenic beauty. For example, if herbicides are used, visitors may object to what they see as poisoning of the environment. Considerations of cost, nutrient cycling, erosion control, and other matters may lead to a choice of management actions that are scenically non-optimal. If this is the case, managers are advised to provide interpretation to the visitors to explain the necessity and temporary nature of the environmental disruption.

One of the major conclusions from our research over the years is that visual effects do not increase or decrease steadily with changes in the physical environment. Instead, scenic beauty often behaves in a marginal utility manner. A small amount of damage, for example, causes rapid declines in perceived scenic beauty, after which additional damage has little negative effect. Therefore, it is possible that a small amount of vegetation management on certain vistas might significantly raise their scenic beauty, while extensive and costly work at heavily overgrown sites may provide little improvement in visitor satisfaction. While we cannot be more specific in our suggestions, we would advise parkway management to inventory vista scenic resources to determine sites where investment in vegetation management might provide the greatest returns.

A second general suggestion emerging from our research is that in scenic beauty, one can have "too much of a good thing." As noted in Part I of this chapter, jagged mountains and large urban trees contribute to scenic beauty but apparently only up to some point, after which additional increments lead to declines in scenic beauty. As to foreground vegetation on the Blue Ridge Parkway, as a general rule the more open the vista the better. However, carried to an extreme, this management guideline might well be counter-productive. A certain amount of foreground vegetation provides vista framing or perhaps is attractive in itself, as with flowering shrubs or plants that attract birds. Lawn-like vista foregrounds might be viewed as unnatural, and this might become even more of a liability if public preference for unmodified nature increases in the future. Some mixture of enclosed and open vistas might be sought in an effort to promote landscape diversity, generally regarded as central to quality visual experiences.

Finally, decisions about vista vegetation management should be framed within the larger context of the Blue Ridge Parkway visual environment and visitor behavior. Whether or not encroaching foreground vegetation at any one vista should be removed depends on the array of other vistas available in a region, and how "regions" are defined should be based in part on patterns of visitation.

In the final analysis, responsibility for making such choices rests with the managers. Science, such as that reported in this article, can support and inform managerial judgments, but it cannot replace it. To be successful, park and forest landscape management must take into account the unique blend of natural environmental features, man-made developments, and visitor attitudes and behavior found at particular sites. Science seeks generalizable truths and necessarily simplifies the world to study it. At the same time, scientific research has the great strength of objectivity and the potential for altering the basic mindsets managers bring to their work. If public wildland resources are to produce the stream of social benefits they are capable of producing, managers and scientists must continue to seek ways of working together.

REFERENCES

Arthur, L.M. 1977. Predicting scenic beauty of forest environments: Some empirical tests. *Forest Science* 23(2): 151–160.

Belsley, D.A., E. Kuh, and R. E. Welsch. 1980. *Regression Diagnostics: Identifying Influential Data and Sources of Collinearity.* New York: John Wiley and Sons.

Brush, R.O., and J. F. Palmer. 1979. Measuring the impact of urbanization on scenic quality: Land use change in the northeast. *Proceedings of Our National Landscape: A Conference on Applied Techniques for Analysis and Management of the Visual Resource*. Berkeley, CA: USDA Forest Service, p. 358–364.

Buhyoff, G.J., L. K. Arndt, and D. B. Propst. 1981. Interval scaling of landscape preference by direct and indirect methods. *Landscape Planning* 8(3): 257–267.

Buhyoff, G.J., L. Gauthier,, and J. D. Wellman. 1984. Predicting scenic quality for urban forests using vegetation measurements. *Forest Science* 30(1): 71–82.

Buhyoff, G.J., and W. A. Leuschner. 1978. Estimating psychological disutility from damaged forest stands. *Forest Science* 24(2): 424–432.

Buhyoff, G.J., W. A. Leuschner, and L. K. Arndt. 1980. The replication of a scenic preference function. *Forest Science* 26(2): 227–230.

Buhyoff, G. J., and M. F. Riesenman. 1979. Experimental manipulation of dimensionality in landscape preference judgments: A quantitative validation. *Leisure Sciences: An Interdisciplinary Journal* 2(3): 221–238.

Buhyoff, G.J., and J. D. Wellman. 1979. Seasonality bias in landscape preference research. *Leisure Sciences* 2(2): 181–190

Buhyoff, G.J. , and J. D. Wellman. 1979. The specification of a non-linear psychophysical function for visual landscape dimensions. *Journal of Leisure Research* 12(3): 157–172.

Buhyoff, G.J., J. D. Wellman, H. Harvey, and R. A. Fraser. 1978. Landscape architects' interpretations of people's landscape preferences. *Journal of Environmental Management* 6(3): 255–262.

Buhyoff, G.J., J. D. Wellman, and T. C. Daniel. 1982. Predicting scenic quality for mountain pine beetle and western spruce budworm damaged forest vistas. *Forest Science* 28(4): 827–838.

Daniel, T.C., and R.C. Boster. 1976. Measuring landscape esthetics; scenic beauty estimation method. USDA Forest Service, Rocky Mtn. Forest and Range Experiment Station. Fort Collins, CO. 66pp.

Draper, N.R., and H. Smith. 1981. *Applied Regression Analysis*. New York: John Wiley and Sons.

Ebel, R.L. 1981. Estimation of the reliability of ratings. *Psychometrica* 16: 407–423.

Feimer, N.R. 1983. Environmental perception and cognition in rural contexts. In A.W. Childs and G.B. Melton (Eds.), *Rural Psychology*. New York: Plenum Press, 113–149.

Feimer, N.R., R.C. Smardon, and K.H. Craik. 1981. Evaluating the effectiveness of observer-based visual resource and impact assessment methods. *Landscape Research* 6: 12–16.

Gauthier, Laureen J. 1981. An Investigation of Preferences for Urban Vegetation through Multidimensional and Unidimensional scaling techniques. M.S. Thesis. Virginia Polytechnic Institute and State University, Blacksburg, VA. 191 pp.

Gazzaniga, M.S. 1970. *The Bisected Brain*. New York: Appleton.

Green, D.M., and J. A. Swetts. 1966. *Signal Detection and Psychophysics*. New York: John Wiley and Sons.

Guilford, J.P. 1954. *Psychometric Methods*. New York: McGraw-Hill.

Gur, R.E., R. C. Gur, and B. Marshalek. 1975. Classroom seating and functional brain asymmetry. *Journal of Educational Psychology* 67: 151–153.

Harcum, E.R. 1978. Lateral dominance as a determinant of temporal order of responding. *In* M. Kinsbourne (Ed.) *Assymetrical Function of the Brain*. Cambridge: Cambridge University Press.

Harvey, H. 1977. *Landscape Preference Quantification: A Comparison of Methods*. Unpublished M.S. Thesis, Virginia Polytechnic Institute and State University, Blacksburg, VA. 110pp.

Heron, W. 1957. Perception as a function of retinal locus and attention. *American Journal of Psychology* 70: 38–48.

Hull, R. Bruce, IV. 1984. Simulation and Evaluation of Scenic Beauty Temporal Distributions in Southern Pine Stands. Ph.D. Dissertation, Virginia Polytechnic Institute and State University, Blacksburg, VA. 159p.

Hull, R.B., G. J. Buhyoff, and T. C. Daniel. 1984. Measurement of scenic beauty: the law of comparative judgment and scenic beauty estimation procedures. *Forest Science* 30(4): 1084–1096.

Kaplan, R. 1973. Predictors of environmental preference: Designers and clients. *In* W.F.E. Preiser (Ed.) *Environmental Design Research*. Stroudsburg, PA: Dowden, Hutchinson & Ross.

Kaplan, R. 1975. Some methods and strategies in the prediction of preference. *In* E.H. Zube, R.O. Brush, and J.G. Fabos (Eds.), *Landscape Assessment: Values, Perceptions, and Resources*. Stroudsburg, PA: Dowden, Hutchinson, and Ross.

Kaplan, S., R. Kaplan, and J. S. Wendt. 1972. Rated preference and complexity for natural and urban visual materials. *Perception and Psychophysics* 12: 354–356.

Lien, J.N., G. J. Buhyoff, and J. D. Wellman. 1984. Development and operationalization of visual preference models for urban forest management. Final Report. U.S.D.A. Forest Service, North Central Forest Experiment Station. Chicago, IL. 32p.

Montgomery, D. C., and E. A. Peck. 1982. *Introduction to Linear Regression Analysis*. New York: John Wiley & Sons.

Patsfall, M. R., N. R. Feimer, G. J. Buhyoff, and J. D. Wellman. 1984. The prediction of scenic beauty from landscape content and composition. *Journal of Environmental Psychology* 11: 7–26.

Propst, D. B., and G. J. Buyoff. 1981. Policy capturing and landscape preference quantification: a methodological study. *Journal of Environmental Management* 11: 45–59.

Shafer, E.L., Jr., J. F. Hamilton, Jr., and E. A. Schmidt. 1969. Natural landscape preferences: a predictive mode. *Journal of Leisure Research* 1(1): 1–10.

Thurstone, L.L. 1927. A law of comparative judgment. *Psychological Review* 34: 273–286.

Togerson, W. S. 1958. *Theory and Methods of Scaling*. New York: Wiley.

Vodak, M. C., P. L. Roberts, J. D. Wellman, and G. J. Buyoff. 1985. Scenic impacts of eastern hardwood management. *Forest Science* 31(2): 289–301.

Weinstein, N. D. 1976. The statistical prediction of environmental preferences. *Environment and Behavior* 8: 611–626.

Wickelgren, L.W. 1967. Convergence in the human newborn. *Journal of Experimental Child Psychology* 5: 74–85.

Wohlwill, J.F. 1968. Amount of stimulus exploration and preference as differential functions of stimulus complexity. *Preference and Psychophysics* 4: 307–312.

Wohlwill, J.F. 1976. Environmental aesthetics: the environment as a source of affect. *In* I. Altman and J.F. Wohnwill (Eds.). *Human Behavior and Environment: Advances in Theory and Research. Vol. 1*. New York: Plenum Press.

Wohlwill, J.F., and G. Harris. 1980. Response to congruity or contrast for man-made features in natural recreation settings. *Leisure Sciences* 3: 349–365.

Zube, E. 1976. Perception of landscape and land use. *In* I. Altman and J.F. Wohlwill (Eds.). *Human Behavior and Environment: Advances in Theory and Research*. Vol. 1. New York: Plenum Press.

Zube, E.H., J. L. Sells, and J. G. Taylor. 1982. Landscape perception: research, application and theory. *Landscape Planning* 9:1–33.

Chapter Six
The Use of Interpretation to Gain Visitor Acceptance of Vegetation Management

Robert H. Becker
Clemson University
Clemson, South Carolina

F. Dominic Dottavio
National Park Service
Atlanta, Georgia

Barbara L. McDonald
Institute of Community and Area Development
Athens, Georgia

To what extent can the images and preferences of landscapes be modified? To answer this question, we examined the effect of a message promoting unmowed roadsides on the visitor's preference for mowed and unmowed scenes along the Blue Ridge Parkway. Apart from the actual responses of visitors to the survey, this chapter also discusses the role of interpretation toward shaping opinion and producing desirable management outputs.

Building Images

Because interpretation is a visitor service used by a variety of personnel in a wide array of settings, there are many definitions of the term. The objectives of interpretation, according to Sharp (1982), are to assist the visitor, to accomplish management goals, and to promote public understanding and appreciation. As Machlis and Field (1984) note, the essence of interpretation is far more difficult to describe. To attempt to describe the "essence" of interpretation, Machlis and Field turned to Tilden's *Interpreting Our Heritage*. Tilden contends that the method of interpretation is to reveal "a larger truth that lies behind any statement of fact." Ashbaugh (1972) expands this presentation of a truth to include interpretation affecting the behavior and attitudes of the visitor.

The use of interpretation as a device for altering behavior and shaping opinions and attitudes has the potential for mischief. Questions involving visitor manipulation and the espousing of specific values are certain to raise questions about the role of the National Park Service.

Regardless of whether or not actions are directed toward gaining visitor support for Park Service management objectives, Park Service management actions project a message about the environment. For example, previous mowing patterns along the Blue Ridge Parkway presented the parkway as having a well-manicured, lawn-like roadside. Through photographic presentations and direct experience, visitors saw and expected the parkway to appear "neat." The Park Service had introduced change and had altered the message of the environment without interpreting the values of the "new message."

As Boulding (1957) points out, "The image is built up as a result of all past experience of the possessor of the image. Part of the image is history itself." He distinguishes the message as information which structures the experience. "The meaning of the message," according to Boulding, "is the change which it produces in the image." Images held by participants may affect their behavior (Becker, 1981a; Schreyer and Roggenbuck, 1979) and their enjoyment and satisfaction (Schreyer and Roggenbuck, 1979; Becker, 1979). Thus, when the message regarding roadside mowing was altered, the initial reaction was to reject the new image in favor of the old image, which had been established over time. Thus, visitors complained.

Images and the values people associate with those images need not be based on reality. Hodgson and Thayer (1980) examined a hypothesis that landscapes that purported to be natural would be given greater value by observers than landscapes that were given attributes with human-implied influences. The authors presented identical photographs to groups in three locations. Within the set of photographs, there were four experimental photographs. Half the group received photographs labeled "pond," "stream bank," "lake," and "forest"; half received photographs labeled "irrigation," "road cut," "reservoir," and "tree farm." Though the experimental photos were identical, subjects ranked the photos having human-implied influences lower than the photos with natural labels.

Becker (1980, 1981b) conducted an experiment with visitors to islands on the upper Mississippi River. Two sets of questionnaires were developed and distributed to island visitors. One set of questionnaires labeled the islands as "sand bars," natural areas along the river; the second set of questionnaires labeled the islands as "dredge spoil sites," the result of channel maintenance by the U.S. Army Corps of Engineers (the islands were, in fact, dredge spoil sites). When the islands were referenced as sand bars, they received a higher visitor preference rating than when classified as dredge spoil sites. While this finding was not particularly exciting, the relationship of this difference to other issues on the questionnaire was interesting. In addition to site evaluation, visitors were asked their opinions regarding the proper management function by the Corps of Engineers. Visitors who received the question with the "sand bar" phrasing were significantly more antagonistic to dredging along the upper Mississippi than were visitors given the "dredge spoil" phrasing.

As Boulding (1957) pointed out, when a new message confronts an image, that message may be rejected, but it will likely engender a conflict between the cognition of the image as held and the image as modified by the new information. Aronson (1976) termed the state of tension that occurs when a person holds two inconsistent cognitions as *cognitive dissonance*. This theory postulates that dissonance is uncomfortable, and as such, the individual will be motivated to reduce dissonance when it occurs. Using the upper Mississippi example, the reduction of dissonance may have occurred when the Corps of Engineers was seen as the creator of a favorite beach rather than its despoiler; however, the individual's value of the site was reduced.

The ability to effect change in an image is tied to the ability to modify an individual's opinions, attitudes, and beliefs. Katz (1960) stated that attitudes serve four functions: understanding, need satisfaction, ego-defense, and value expression. If an attitude serves multiple functions, it becomes more difficult to alter. This is consistent with Boulding's belief that images that have been developed with a broad base of reinforcement are less likely to change as a result of new messages. Rokeach (1971) and Boulanger and Smith (1973) agreed that significant changes in attitudes and values rarely occur as a result of short presentations. Thus, if a persuasive presentation effects a change in visitor response toward park management objectives, then the attitudes upon which visitor responses were based are probably not closely tied to the individual's self-perception.

The ethical issue of modifying visitor opinions and attitudes is, to some extent, answered by the relative stability of closely held attitudes and values. The issue of trying to effect change, however, should be grounded in the purpose and goals of the National Park System.

Reduced mowing along the Blue Ridge Parkway to stimulate wildflowers and increase native vegetation diversity is consistent with the idea of national parks' providing a setting with minimum influence by man. In addition to philosophical reasons for altering roadside mowing, savings in maintenance dollars and energy costs also appeared to influence the decision to alter mowing practices.

Methods

The study reported in this chapter had certain imposed limitations. First, because of the cost involved in preparing the final questionnaire, only one "treatment" message could be tested. Therefore, it was not possible to examine the different effects of a negative message, an emotional message, and an economic rationale message. The message developed was based on information from the existing marketing research literature. While the pilot instrument used large paired photographs with no written statement interpreting them, the final questionnaires used photos that were much smaller and were labeled by a caption and a rating scale below each photograph.

The communication for the pilot of this study was a written brochure with a cover page that carried the interpretive message (intended to bias the respondent toward favoring less mowing and shaggier roadside) as the treatment, a paragraph of instructions directing the respondent to select the photograph he preferred, and a set of ten paired 5" × 7" color photographs depicting mowed and unmowed scenes along the Blue Ridge Parkway (see Appendix B).

The interpretive message for this study involved two concepts which were expected to influence visitors to the Blue Ridge Parkway. First, the concept of natural beauty attempted to define a norm associating the parkway with being "natural." The idea that mowing threatens this concept was also presented. The second concept was to stress the amount of money saved if mowing were reduced. This rationalistic argument was introduced to reference mowing as not only a threat to the concept of a "natural" roadside along the Blue Ridge Parkway, but a threat which was human-induced and human-controlled. The message was reinforced with a series of three pictures showing a scene in transition from highly manicured to "natural" or unmowed. The portion of the message tied to natural, unmowed qualities was cited from Aldo

Leopold's *A Sand County Almanac*. This reference to a familiar authority was intended to make the emotional argument the proper orientation for parkway visitors. Finally, to tie the two concepts together, we developed a catch phrase—"There is an economy in natural things"—as the closing line on the interpretive message. (The messages given to the treatment study groups are shown in Appendix B).

The message was pilot tested with students at Clemson University using 10 pairs of photographs. Sixty students in three classes were given the instrument. Thirty booklets had the interpretive message, and 30 did not. The students were asked to examine each pair of photographs and check the one they most preferred. Each respondent, therefore, identified 10 photographs with each of the two groups having 30 total selections. Figure 6.1 is a graph of the photographs with lower

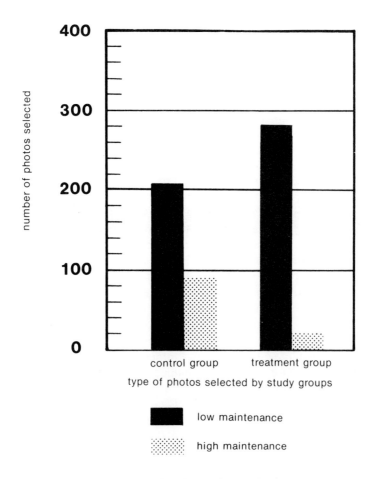

Figure 6.1.   Preference for roadside maintenance.

maintenance. The treatment group preferred the low maintenance photos at a ratio of 1.37:1 over the control group, possibly because of the presence of wildflowers in a number of photographs. Based upon this pilot test, the interpretive message was forwarded to the University of Tennessee for inclusion in an on-site study of visitor attitudes toward vegetation management on the Blue Ridge Parkway.

The field study used a photo-questionnaire containing a series of 18 photo-pairs of scenes photographed over the last 30 years along the Blue Ridge Parkway. The study used eight pairs of photographs contrasting various degrees of roadside mowing and 10 pairs depicting burning, shrub removal, and tree removal. A number of photos were modified by scientists of the State University of New York at Syracuse to simulate various stages of tree and shrub growth. A detailed description of the field application is given in Chapter 1.

A chi-square analysis was used to test for association between respondents' preferences for specific photographs and exposure to the interpretive message and to test for association between respondents' stated opinions regarding vegetation management practices and their exposure to the interpretive message.

Results

Tables 6.1 and 6.2 give the scores for the analysis of photographs. The only significant associations involved photographs depicting mowing practices. None of the respondents' reactions to photographs involving burning, shrub removal, or tree removal was affected by the introduction of the interpretive message. One photo in six of the eight mowing pairs was affected by the interpretive message. In one pair both photos were affected. Of the eight mowing photographs showing significant association, six involved high intensity maintenance, and two involved low intensity maintenance. The pattern of association followed the results of the Clemson pilot study. Respondents exposed to the brief interpretive message exhibited less approval of and less preference for the photos showing more mowing than for photos showing less mowing.

Similar results were found through the analysis of the vegetation management survey. The only statements associated with the interpretive message dealt with mowing. Among the mowing statements only those suggesting intensive mowing prompted significantly different responses between the two groups. Weekly mowing, mowing every two weeks or when the grasses are 3 to 6 in. tall, mowing from the road's edge to the ditch or swale, and mowing from the road's edge to the tree line had significantly less support from the group exposed to the interpretive message. Management alternatives suggesting less intensive mowing regimes exhibited no significant difference between the

Table 6.1. Chi-square values for the presence of the interpretive message and preference for vegetation management practices as depicted by the photo questionnaire[1] (see Appendix B).

Photo#	Photo Caption	Chi-Square Value
1a	No mowing beyond guardrail	1.62 N.S.
1b	Mowing to and beyond guardrail	.57 N.S.
2a	Mowed one mower width from roadside	2.57 N.S.
2b	Mowed to treeline	10.79 *
3a	No mowing	4.26 N.S.
3b	Complete mowing into treeline	9.92 *
4a	Vegetation not mowed around sign	7.36 *
4b	Vegetation mowed around & beyond sign	15.90 *
5a	Shrub vegetation in near foreground	.10 N.S.
5b	Shrubs managed by controlled burning	.37 N.S.
6a	Mowed one mower width from roadside	2.93 N.S.
6b	Mowing complete to treeline	12.94 *
7a	Mowing to treeline	6.61 *
7b	Mowed one mower width from roadside.	1.79 N.S.
8a	Mowed only at mid-summer	21.68 *
8b	Mowed every three weeks	5.39 N.S.
9a	Only roadside shoulder mowed	1.56 N.S.
9b	Mowed to fenceline and beyond	6.60 *
10a	Trees closing in the scenic vista	2.25 N.S.
10b	Low shrubs in distant foreground	3.67 N.S.
11a	Vista with some trees in foreground	1.81 N.S.
11b	Trees removed from foreground in vista	.76 N.S
12a	Foreground trees in vista	1.74 N.S.
12b	No foreground trees in vista	1.51 N.S.
13a	Scene with foreground trees	2.87 N.S.
13b	Foreground trees completely removed	2.66 N.S.
14a	Hardwood and conifer (evergreen) trees present	4.41 N.S.
14b	Hardwoods cut to emphasize conifers	2.43 N.S.
15a	Shrubs in foreground	.49 N.S.
15b	Shrubs removed by cutting & controlled burning	1.64 N.S.
16a	Trees closing in vista more than 50%	3.09 N.S.
16b	Selective cutting to re-open vista	1.47 N.S.
17a	Low shrubs in distant foreground	2.38 N.S.
17b	Mowing and cutting of foreground vegetation	2.63 N.S.
18a	Original scene with edge trees	1.56 N.S.
18b	Single edge tree removed	1.74 N.S.

[1]For photo analysis the cells were collapsed into:
"not at all"
"a little" and "somewhat"
"quite a bit" and "very much"

* Indicates significance beyond the Alpha .05 level.

Table 6.2. Chi-square values for the presence of the interpretive message and preference for vegetation management practices as depicted by the seven point scale questionnaire (see Appendix B).

Descriptive Item	X^2 Value 6 df
I. The roadside grass should be mowed:	
1. weekly, like a lawn	14.69 *
2. every two weeks, when 3-6 inches tall	13.40 *
3. once per month, when at least 10 inches tall	5.57 N.S.
4. once in the Fall after the wildflowers are through blooming	11.24 N.S.
5. only one mower width (7 feet) from the edge of the road surface	3.79 N.S.
6. two mower widths (14 feet) from the road's edge	11.25 N.S.
7. from the road's edge to the ditch or swale	13.67 *
8. from the road's edge to the treeline	23.77 *
9. as little as possible, only when necessary to maintain driver safety and help prevent grass fires	10.53 N.S.
II. Shrubs and trees at pull-off vistas should be cut or trimmed:	
10. annually to maintain a completely clear view	8.07 N.S.
11. every 5 to 7 years, before the shrubs in the foreground block much of the view	9.19 N.S.
12. just often enough so that no more than ⅓ of the view is blocked	5.66 N.S.

* Indicates significance beyond the Alpha .05 level.

two respondent groups. Examples of alternative regimes are as follows: mowing when the grass was taller than 10 in., once in the fall after the wildflowers have bloomed, only one or two mower widths from the road's edge, and mowing as little as possible and then only to maintain driver safety.

Discussion

Since the Clemson pilot test involved photographs depicting only mowed and unmowed scenes, the effects of a message supporting less mowing on visitor opinions and preferences toward other vegetation management alternatives were uncertain. We hypothesized that the message would bias the respondent toward a more generalized definition of "natural" and would result in recipients of the message supporting less

less human intervention and a lower intensity of vegetation management. However, this did not occur. The message supporting less mowing activity only affected the respondents' opinions toward mowing.

If interpretive messages can be developed to garner support and shape public opinion toward specific actions without being generalized to other management activities, then potential conflicts created when modifying visitor preferences are minimized. For example, one may wish to reduce mowing for the sake of fuel/dollar savings or of freeing labor support for other activities and still wish to introduce controlled burns to suppress herbaceous vegetation or remove trees to open up vistas. It would not be helpful to introduce a program to increase support for less mowing if it created a negative reaction to desired vegetation management programs. The results from this study suggest that a precise message can achieve specific results.

As previously mentioned, the ability to affect an attitude depends on the importance of that attitude to the individual's self-concept. Attitudes and opinions regarding vegetative management in a national park may not be important to the individual's self-concept, but it may be tied to a person's definition of "natural" and his image of the role of naturalness in park settings. If the interpretive message created a conflict between the image of the Blue Ridge Parkway as having a well groomed roadside and the role of a national park as presenting nature with minimum human influence, that dissonance was reduced through allowing a selective reevaluation of the values of mowing. Proponents of the theory of cognitive dissonance support this form of incremental reduction of tension (Aronson, 1976).

However, what about visitor complaints? Any change will usually draw dissatisfaction from some sectors of the public. If we examine the preferences for mowing practices along the Blue Ridge Parkway, we may gain insight into the intensity of public reaction toward mowing practices. About 12% of the respondents who *did not* receive the interpretive message made statements of "not at all" liking low maintenance mowing photographs. About 34% of the respondents who *did* receive the interpretive message made statements of "not at all" liking high maintenance mowing photographs. If we assume that complaints regarding management of the parkway will come from those expressing a negative rather than a positive opinion, then we stand a 300% greater chance of receiving complaints of intensive roadside mowing from visitors who value a more natural, less-managed roadside. Visitors who were not exposed to the interpretive message were a third less bothered by the natural roadside than the exposed group was toward the manicured roadside. While this comparison is less intense than the difference between the Clemson pilot groups, it is more likely to reflect the realities of visitors' opinions at the Blue Ridge Parkway.

Conclusions

Behavior, according to Boulding (1957), depends on the image that is formed from messages interpreted by the individual. In this light, interpretation is a powerful tool. An interpretive program not only enriches the experience of the visitor to the park but also explains the management roles of the National Park Service.

The results of this study and the previous work by Burris-Bammel (1978); Geller et al. (1982); Oliver et al. (1985), and others suggest that information has the capacity to modify attitudes and opinions. Given the substantial public investment in the maintenance and operation of the National Park System, it would be prudent to implement a public information program to market specific Park Service programs. The National Park Service should take its cue from the private sector: marketing an image can reinforce a desired image. The images can build constituent support, reduce unnecessary conflict, and produce a greater visitor understanding of the objectives of the National Park Service.

REFERENCES

Aronson, R. 1976. *The Social Animal.* New York: Freeman Press.

Ashbaugh, B. L. 1972. New interpretive methods and techniques. *In* Schoenfeld, C. (Ed.) *Interpreting Environmental Issues.* Madison, WI: Dembar Educational Research Services, Inc., 1972.

Becker, R. H. 1979. Travel compatibility on the upper Mississippi River. *Journal of Travel Research* 18(1): 33–41.

Becker, R. H. 1980. Dredged spoil: an identity problem, not a terminology problem. *Journal of Environmental Education* 12:1.

Becker, R. H. 1981a. User reaction to wild and scenic river designation. *Water Resources Bulletin* 17(4): 623–26.

Becker, R. H. 1981b. Displacement of recreational users between the lower St. Croix and upper Mississippi Rivers. *Journal of Environmental Management* 13(4):259–267.

Boulanger, F. D., and J. P. Smith. 1973. Educational principles and techniques for interpreters. USDA Forest Service Tech. Report, PNW-9, Portland, OR.

Boulding, K. E. 1957. *The Image.* Ann Arbor, MI: The University of Michigan Press.

Burris-Bammel, L. L. 1978. Information's effect on attitude: a longitudinal study. *Journal of Environmental Education* 9(4): 41–50.

Geller, E. S., R. A. Winett, and P. B. Everett. 1982. *Preserving the Environment: New Strategies for Behavior Change*. New York: Pergamon Press.

Hodgson, R. W., and R. L. Thayer. 1980. Implied human influences reduce landscape beauty. *Landscape Planning* 7:171–179.

Jacob, G. 1977. Conflict in outdoor recreation—the search for understanding. *Utah Tourism and Recreation Review* 6(4):1–5.

Katz, D. 1960. The functional approach to the study of attitudes. *Public Opinion Quarterly* 6:248–268.

Leopold, A. 1984. *A Sand County Almanac*. New York: Ballantine Books.

Machlis, G. E., and D. R. Field. 1984. *On Interpretation*. Corvallis, OR: Oregon St. University Press.

Oliver, S. S., J. W. Roggenbuck, and A. E. Watson. 1985. Education to reduce impacts in forest campgrounds. *Journal of Forestry* 83(4): 234–236.

Rokeach, M. 1971. Long-range experimental modification of values, attitudes, and behavior. *American Psychology* 26(5):453–459.

Schreyer, R., and J. Roggenbuck. 1979. Visitor images of national parks: the influence of social definitions of place upon perceptions and behavior. Paper presented at the Second Conf. on Scientific Research in the National Parks, Nov. 28.

Sharp, G. 1982. *Interpreting the Environment*. New York: John Wiley and Sons.

Tilden, F. 1967. *Interpreting Our Heritage*. Chapel Hill, NC: The University of North Carolina Press.

Chapter Seven
Historical Overview and Landscape Classification of Vistas and Rural Landscapes Along the Blue Ridge Parkway

Richard C. Smardon, Timothy R. Day,
James F. Palmer, Tad Redway, and Lawrence Reichardt
State University of New York
Syracuse, New York

This chapter reports on two different contributions of the State University of New York (SUNY) College of Environmental Science and Forestry to the Blue Ridge Parkway study. The first is a brief historical analysis of vegetation management practices along the Blue Ridge area by people living there at different periods of time. Second, a professionally derived biophysical landscape classification system is presented and compared with Hammitt's perceptual classification described in Chapter 2. This classification is used to assess how representative particular scenes are of the overall set of scenes of the Blue Ridge Parkway.

Historic Vegetative Management Practices

Introduction to Historic Analysis

The initial construction funds for the Blue Ridge Parkway were allocated under the authority of the National Industrial Recovery Act of

June 13, 1933. An act establishing the parkway under administration of the National Park Service was passed by Congress on June 30, 1936 (see Land Tenure Chart, Table 7.1). The idea of a Blue Ridge Parkway first began prior to World War I, but the concept of a scenic road connecting Shenandoah and Great Smoky Mountains National Parks developed mostly during the Great Depression.

One of the prime goals then, as well as today, was to provide Americans with a living museum of natural and manmade form. The problem in pursuing this goal lay in the difficulty of maintaining the open quality along the Blue Ridge. Rapid vegetal growth from highly conducive environmental conditions can eventually block the visitors' view from the road.

The purpose of this section is to present (1) a clear picture of the most historically significant cultures of the Blue Ridge settlement, (2) the land management techniques used by native Americans and settlers, and (3) the relationship of these techniques, where applicable, to the management practices of the National Park Service today.

Blue Ridge Culture and Management Practices

The first known party to have explored the Blue Ridge Mountain area was DeSoto in 1560, followed by the Brickell Party in the 1730s (Smathers, 1982). In addition to finding Indians inhabiting the area, these explorers found a pristine landscape enscribed as "beautiful valleys covered with woods, pastures, and savannas" (see Land Tenure Chart, Table 7.1). They also found an extensive trail system developed by the Indians, particularly on the slopes and summits where they set up summer camps. Some evidence indicates that camp sites, referred to as "balds," still exist today because of their intensive use by Indians and later settlers (Mitchell, 1848; see Figures 7.1 and 7.2).

By 1850 the Blue Ridge was sparsely settled in isolated family farming units (see Figure 7.3). The land, like most of the South and Northeast at this time, was managed as large, irregular-shaped gardens rather than fields. Hillsides were cleared by girdling and burning for pasturing sheep, cattle, and mules (Stilgoe, 1982; see Figures. 7.2 and 7.3). In 1848 Mitchell explains that in addition to the Indian summer encampment, over-grazing may explain the "bald" formations.

Most of the early mountaineers were agrarian. Consequently, the process of finding suitable lands for farming and pasturing involved the analysis of vegetative cover where scrub, grasslands, and coniferous trees indicated poor soils; hickory, walnuts, oaks, and honey locust indicated very fertile soils; chestnut indicated gravelly soils; and sycamore, red elm, and birch indicated loose valley soils (Stilgoe, 1982).

Among the early mountaineers, the Scot/Irish (see Land Tenure Chart, Table 7.1) rapidly adopted the Indian ways of cultivation. They used the simple technique of slash and burn but with no replenishment of the soil (Riddel, 1974). Following the Germans, they settled first in the bottom lands where soil and game were best. They seemed to prefer soils underlain by shale and avoided limestone altogether. However, after they moved into the smaller coves where the soil was shallower, widespread erosion led the U.S. Department of Agriculture (USDA) to proclaim 100,000 farms unfit for agriculture (Jolley, 1969).

Unlike the Scot/Irish, the Germans' goal was to own the land and manage it efficiently. They laid out and built barns and out-buildings in an orderly cluster separated from the house to maximize economy of effort. They chose land heavily timbered in hardwoods in valleys composed of limestone soils similar to their homeland (Long, 1972). They planted small gardens in which they grew vegetables, including beets, parsnips, radishes, carrots, leeks, cauliflower, parsley, asparagus, cucumbers, and peas. In addition, they usually planted orchards of fruit trees in the first cleared field. The Germans consolidated some of the abandoned cleared patches left by the Scot/Irish, and following their European traditions, allowed cattle and sheep to graze to subdue the land for several years prior to cultivation. After a period of intense tillage, crops were planted and rotated, followed by more manuring to increase its fertility. Cattle were routinely allowed to free-range after the fields became permanent.

Management Techniques

Each of these cultures—Indians, Scot/Irish, and Germans—carried its own land management ideas into the Blue Ridge, and each has determined how the Blue Ridge looks today. Our research indicates four major categories of utilization/management. They were sometimes used alone but most often in combination with other techniques.

Girdling. The most prevalent form of vegetative management during the mid-1800s to early 1900s was girdling, which was used primarily by the Scot/Irish. The technique involves simply removing a band or belt of a tree's bark and cambium layer inhibiting the flow of moisture and nutrients to the upper stems. The point in girdling is to eliminate the shade-producing canopy of the tree without removing the entire tree. This allowed grasses to grow for forage or cultivation.

Slash Burning. The goal of this German technique was to super-enrich the soil. Deciduous trees were felled in summer, and conifers were felled in winter. The limbs and slabs were then piled evenly across the ground and fired, singeing the soil. Then rye was planted and harvested. More limbs were spread and fired followed by a planting of grains. The technique was repeated every five or six years. A by-

Table 7.1. Land Tenure Chronology.

Period	Geographic Location	Land Tenure Practice	Ethnic Group	Source(s)
Late 1600's	Virginia and Carolinas	plantation settlement, extensive agricultural practice, free-ranch of livestock, crude structures, cash cropping	English w/Scot/Irish servants	Stilgoe (1982)
Pre-1716	Shenandoah Valley	timber burned to increase game habitats	Native Americans	Kercheval (1902)
Early 1700's	Appalachia	tree girdling, rough plowing between dead stands	Scot/Irish	Kercheval (1902)
1718 Stilgoe (1982)	Pennsylvania Great Valley North Carolina Piedmont and Blue Ridge	small patch farming; trees girdled—left standing or burned, corn and tobacco crops	Scot/ Irish	Graeff (1941) Opie (1980) Kercheval (1902)
1775	North Carolina	German movement continues from Pennsylvania into western counties and highlands of North Carolina	Germans	Bittenger (1901)
1776	Blue Ridge North Carolina	Blue Ridge and Alleghenys open up for settlement by continental colonies		
1700's	Pennsylvania	permanent meadows were plowed, pasturing occurred May 1–Nov. 1, vegetable gardening on warm side of house, neatly fenced; efficient farm practices, tilled intensively, rotated crops, manured farmstead kept orderly and clean; frequently cattle and sheep turned into newly cut overland to subdue it for cultivation, prevailing practice was to pasture livestock on	Germans	Long (1972)

Period	Region	Description	Settlers	Reference
1700's	Pennsylvania	wornout field reverting to succession; fewer farmers laid down land in grass after taking two to four grain crops, upland meadows pastured several years before reverting to crop rotation; apple orchards common fences symbolize good farming	German	Rush (1875) Long (1972)
1700–1800's	North Carolina and Toe Valley	German farm distinguished from Scot/Irish by superior size of barns, plain compact form of houses, height of enclosures, extent of orchards, fertility of fields, luxuriousness of meadows, appearance of plenty and order	Scot/ Irish	Sheppard (1936)
1700–1800's	Appalachia	naturalist Andre Michaux taught valley settlers how to prepare wild ginseng for the Chinese market	Scot/ Irish	Weller (1965)
1700–1800's	Appalachia	houses built on bottom lands near streams; slopes farmed (called perpendicular farming)	Scot/ Irish	Kollmorgen (1942)
1700–1800's	Appalachia	unfamiliar with manuring or soil conditioning; hillside patches cleared as lower fields depleted	Scot/ Irish	Weller (1965) Stilgoe (1982) Sheppard (1935)
1700–1800's	Appalachia	principal crops, corn and tobacco	Scot/ Irish	
Mid-Late 1800's	Blue Ridge North Carolina	exploitation by lumber and mining companies result in large tracts of cut-out, burned-out, washed-out lands; feldspar and mica primarily, small operations.	Scot/ Irish	Sheppard (1935)
1935	Blue Ridge North Carolina	area consolidated and bought by U.S. Forest Service		Smathers (1982)
1952-Present	Blue Ridge	governance by National Park Service		Smathers (1982)

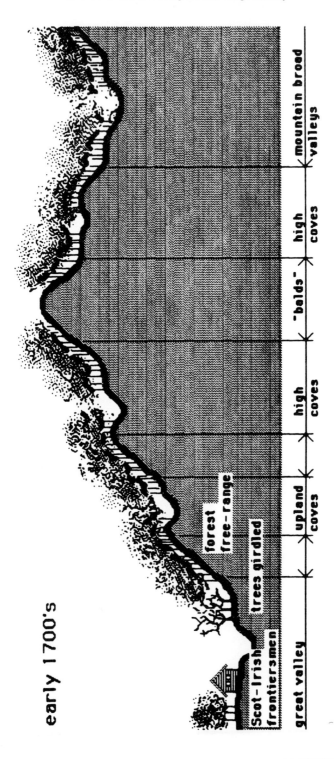

Figure 7.1.   Land use patterns in the Blue Ridge Mountains in the early 1700s.

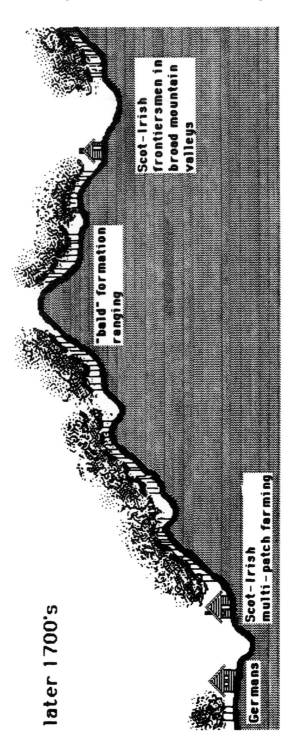

Figure 7.2.   Land use patterns in the Blue Ridge Mountains in the late 1700s.

Figure 7.3. Land use patterns in the Blue Ridge Mountains in the 1800s.

product of burning was the resumption of successful growth. Large areas called "colicks" were formed after the fields became deficient and even today are composed of a dominant cover of compact heath shrubs.

Grazing. The early settlers raised a variety of domestic animals, including sheep, cattle, and mules. Because of the thinness of the upland soils, evidence indicates that many of the so-called "grassy" balds were maintained and extended by constant trampling. The succeeding grasses, mostly mountain oat grass (*Danthonia ompressa*) and the species *Rumex acetosella*, outcompeted most tree or shrub reproduction (Smathers, 1982).

Natural Selection. The natural selection process is exhibited by the ongoing emergence of plant species. It is seen most dramatically following severe disturbances such as cutting and burning, high winds, or soil erosion. For example, deep erosion can occur on the less fertile subsoils in the margins of old fields. Masses of heath or broomsedge and asters can compete with other grasses, and they usually replace them quickly in the warm months of the year.

Growing in sparse stands, broomsedge (*Andropogon* spp.), for example, survives as a monoculture until enough ground litter is produced to support other grasses and woody vegetation (Baker, 1972). At the time of this writing, the authors have not found enough reference material to indicate the length of time before other pioneering plants outcompete broomsedge on abandoned farmland. However, this native plant appears to have potential applications in a vegetation management policy for the parkway.

Broomsedge is a free-standing, narrow-stalked plant that does not pose the same entangling and overgrown characteristics of kudzu or other exotic woody pioneering plants. It thrives essentially as a monoculture outcompeting other pioneering species for available nutrients. It presents a fine-textured, uniform vegetal mass for an extended period of time. Its maintenance needs are minimal.

Summary

Any vegetative management technique used should be preceded by a thorough analysis of the goals and objectives to be accomplished and the environment in which the technique will take place. The practicality of the Park Service's goal to provide the viewer with a living museum is not discussed here but is taken as a given. Since the primary thrust of our research involved the human cultural aspect of *viewing* from the Blue Ridge Parkway, as discussed in Chapter 8, physical parameters should also be considered.

Basically, viewing from the Blue Ridge Parkway involves two major physical components: the position of the viewer and the scene to be viewed. The viewer position generally means either viewing at a scenic overlook standing or sitting, or viewing along the road while moving in a car. The speed of the car and the road configuration are important also because a view is more likely to be seen on a straight road at slow speed than on a curve. This also means that the amount of vegetation to be managed should be determined not only by what is viewed but also by whether the viewer is moving or standing still.

Once the analysis of physical parameters determines where vegetative management should take place, only techniques that are consistent with these parameters and other goals and objectives should be implemented. While girdling, cutting, and burning could be implemented and rationalized as management methods historically accurate to the Blue Ridge, the visual result of these techniques would probably have little chance of being publicly accepted. Grazing and natural selection, on the other hand, have potential applications.

We learned from parkway managers early in this study that the prime concern along the parkway is keeping vegetation from intruding into a scene. Techniques of controlled burning and cutting or mowing are required not only to keep long vistas open but also to maintain a defense against severe erosion on steep slopes in soils that are often thin, well-drained, and of low fertility.

Although native broomsedge can serve as a visually-enhancing, historically accurate, and maintenance-free method of managing vegetation in areas of disturbed or nutrient-poor soils along the parkway, its universal application is questionable. Preparing roadside land for broomsedge introduction would mean deliberately engaging in poor soil management practices. Cleared land would have to be grubbed and constantly re-cleared, allowing nutrients to leach out of the soil. Serious erosion and sedimentation would no doubt result.

As discussed earlier, one of the environmental results of "cutting and burning" used by the Germans to enrich the soil was the formation of "colicks." Another environmental result found in this study centers on the formation of what is known as the Blue Ridge "balds." While much speculation surrounds the origin of the "balds," many investigators believe they were caused by a combination of intense use by the early settlers, including overgrazing, on thin, fragile soils (Smathers, 1982; Wells, 1937).

The dilemma these examples pose is obvious. The abuse of the soil to control vegetal growth and promote the growth of more compact, self-maintaining plant species may or may not be advisable in all management situations. Additionally, little research exists documenting the process required for the controlled abuse of soil to regulate vegetation height.

Clearly, a more practical approach would be to use specific types of native plants. Basically, they should have characteristics adaptable to the existing environment, including the soil and micro-climate. Their physical characteristics should be compatible to the surrounding vegetal and topographic context of the view. Bailey (1978) classifies the Blue Ridge Parkway area as within the Eastern Deciduous Forest Province of the Hot Continental Division and the Humid Temperate Domain. Perennial vegetation should contain the following characteristics: First, since most soils on steep slopes and ridge lines are thin and low in nutrients, plants should be shallow-rooted, fibrous and able to absorb and hold nutrients for extended periods of time. Second, since the climate is humid and temperate and rainfall is abundant, plants should be able to withstand the potential erosive effects of heavy rainfall, snow, and sedimentation.

Physically, plants should be complementary in terms of form, size, and texture. More importantly, the height of the plant should be self-maintaining and predictable because placement on a given slope with respect to the viewer position is crucial in maintaining the desired view. In most cases, native grasses such as broomsedge could be used in near foreground areas; but if the slope falls away sharply, native shrubs with a stronger root system should be used.

Landscape Classification

Introduction

When asking subjects to respond to certain images delineating vegetative management alternatives, one needs to know how representative these scenes are of the entire Blue Ridge Parkway. Over 250 scenic overlooks have been established along the 470 miles of the parkway. Because of logistical and financial constraints, as well as the tolerance levels of questionnaire respondents (Zeisel, 1981), simulation of vegetation management techniques at every overlook was beyond the scope of this project. Therefore, it became necessary to select several overlook scenes representative of the range of visual experiences encountered along the entire parkway.

To begin this selection process, we obtained a library of Ektachrome slides from the University of Tennessee. The photographic library of 298 slides contained a shot from each of the established parkway overlooks and a number of duplicate photographs made to compensate for poor lighting conditions or technical problems.

Our slide selection process involved four sequential steps:
1. Formulation of a landscape classification system.
2. Classification of each of the slides in the photographic library.
3. Grouping of overlook scenes based on similar landscape components.
4. Selection of 1 or 2 representative slides from each of the established groups of overlook scenes based upon degree of photographic quality and suitability for simulation purposes.

Each of these four steps is explained in greater detail.

Formulation of a Landscape Classification System

The first consideration was to determine the classification methods most appropriate for the grouping and selection of scenes most representative of the variety of overlook scenes along the parkway. A review of the existing literature in visual analysis revealed that several classification systems had been specifically developed for mountainous regions (Elsner and Smardon, 1979). However, most of these were designed to determine relative levels of scenic quality. Clearly, scenic judgments are simply too limited for broadly describing the nature of the distinct landscape types inherent to the Blue Ridge Mountains. Most mountain landscape classifications were formulated for ranges in the western United States. Topographic relationships, vegetation, and atmospheric effects differ dramatically between the eastern and western mountain landscapes. Many of these approaches could be used as references or models, but direct application to the Blue Ridge problem was inappropriate. A classification system would have to be tailored to the specific characteristics of the Blue Ridge Mountains.

A second supposition critical to the development of an appropriate classification method involved the issue of reliability. The system would have to be formulated so that the same results would be produced regardless of who the reviewer was or the number of times the slide library was subjected to examination. Related to this issue was the recurring problem of insuring that objectivity was maintained during classification procedures.

Our classification approach is based on the precept that the visual character of the physical landscape is determined primarily by: (1) the nature of the landscape's topography and (2) the type of natural and/or man-made cover overlying that terrain (Anderson, 1979). The interaction of the form, line, color, and texture of the landforms and the land cover/land-use produce a multitude of visual patterns that can be categorized on the basis of their similarities and distinctions. It is a biophysical classification that may be compared to Hammitt's perceptual classification (Chapter 2).

Most of the documented applications for similar systems have involved classification of physiographic landscapes at a larger regional scale. Although the Blue Ridge Mountains represent one such phys-iographic landscape (North Atlantic Regional Water Resources Commit-tee, 1972), we needed a classification method that would be effective in discerning landscape distinctions at a smaller scale within the Blue Ridge context.

The landscape series/unit framework is essentially a method for ana-lyzing three-dimensional landscape character from a two-dimensional planimetric data base. In addition, the system presumes that the land-scape character will remain essentially similar regardless of where a potential observer stands within the specific series/unit type. Clearly, this assumption is justified when the system is used for general land-scape planning purposes at a larger scale. However, for describing land-scape character from specific observation points with views of three-dimensional space, these assumptions are inappropriate. The work of Gibson (1979), Felleman (1979), Litton (1968), and others indicate that depending on such environmental factors as viewing height, sight line orientation to the landscape, interposition of landforms and objects, as well as factors affecting the mechanics of vision such as distance and atmospheric clarity, landscape elements may not be perceived by the observer as they actually exist. For example, a highly serrated ridgeline with gentle side slopes that is in the background of the observer's pic-ture plane and oriented parallel to the viewer's sight line may, in fact, appear to be a series of steep individual peaks because of the degrada-tion of visible detail occurring with distance and the impact of atmo-spheric effects. Similarly, the spatial enclosure of a valley may be per-ceived to be considerably less than it actually is because of visual reduction of scale occurring as the viewer's height increases above the terrain.

With these basic suppositions in mind, we examined the existing landscape literature in an attempt develop a classification system. Since the slide library revealed a broad spectrum of vegetation types, land uses, and terrain, we determined that the framework of our classifica-tion system should be modeled on the landform series and land use/land cover unit system employed by Anderson (1979), Smardon and Mahon (1980), and the 1972 North Atlantic Regional Water Resources Study (NAR). In an effort to understand the variables affecting percep-tion of three-dimensional landscape character, we developed a series of "form modifiers" that were incorporated into the classification matrix (see Figure 7.4). These form modifiers assumed four basic positions in the system:

1. Viewer position of the overlook scene in context to the surround-ing landscape.

2. Division of the picture plane into three distance zones—fore-ground, midground, and background.

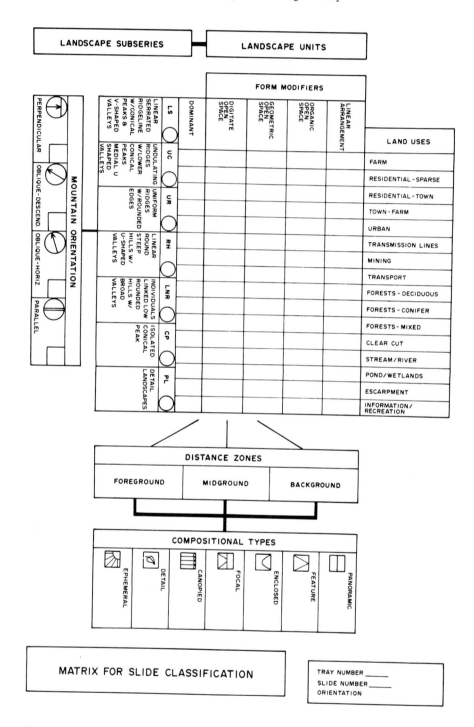

Figure 7.4.   Matrix for slide classification.

3. Established dimensions describing the spatial configuration of objects and open spaces in the land cover/land use units.

4. Axial orientation of terrain to the viewer's sight line in the landform series.

Furthermore, in a three-dimensional viewing experience, the landscape, as a holistic entity, exhibits a particular compositional character. Litton (1968) documented seven specific landscape compositional types that recur among all forested environments which, in turn, are supported by perceptual research findings. Since Litton's compositional classification scheme represented a potential dimension for grouping similar overlook scenes, it was incorporated into our Blue Ridge Classification System as well.

Definition of Components of the Classification System
The finalized classification system, as shown in Figure 7.4, operated on five levels and two sublevels of analysis: (1) viewer position, (2) compositional types, (3) distance zones, (4) land cover units and the sub-unit form modifiers, and (5) landform series and the landform orientation sub-series. For purposes of clarity and potential future application of the system, the criteria for each of the identified dimensions are presented in detail.

Viewer Position. As previously discussed, the observer's position in relation to the landscape view is critical to categorizing the type of visual experience encountered. Adapted directly from Litton's typology, three conditions are recognized (Figure 7.5):

- Viewer inferior—the viewer is essentially below the surrounding landform.
- Viewer normal—an essentially level sight line is maintained by the viewer to survey the landscape.
- Viewer superior—conditions under which the observer's sight line drops below the level sight line to peruse the surrounding terrain.

Compositional Types. Again, Litton's typology was directly applied to this classification section. Each type is only briefly defined here. For a more comprehensive explanation of each type, refer to USDA Forest Research Paper PSW-49 (Litton, 1968).

Panoramic Landscape: Line emphasis in the picture plane is essentially horizontal. View is essentially unbounded; both distance and peripheral vision are unencumbered.

Feature Landscape: Domination of the landscape by a strong visual element(s) (usually vertical) while the remainder of the landscape is visually subordinate.

Figure 7.5.   Viewing positions (after Litton, 1968).

Enclosed Landscape: Counterpart of the feature, this landscape is represented by "bowl-like forms with a continuity of sides around a central base plane."

Focal Landscape: The parallel alignment of lines, objects, or land-forms that appear to converge upon a single focal point at the horizon.

Canopied Landscape: The predominance of views in which the forest upperstory or canopy provides a visual overhead plane.

Detailed Landscape: Scenes of a very small scale in which detailed components such as individual rocks, plants, water, and animal tracks occupy the observer's attention, while the surrounding landscape context is usually not visible.

Ephemeral Landscape: Dynamic, transitory effects that significantly alter or dominate the visual character of the landscape. Weather conditions, atmospheric conditions, light and reflections represent the most common ephemeral effects.

Panoramic, Feature, Focal, Enclosed, and Detailed landscapes constituted the fundamental or larger-scale compositional types identified in the Blue Ridge slide library. Canopied and Ephemeral landscapes usually served as secondary types or compositional qualifiers. As such, any particular scene could be classified by more than one type. An example would be an isolated peak wreathed with a blue atmospheric haze that might be categorized as both a Feature and Ephemeral landscape. This dual classification was not limited to secondary compositional types. In several cases during pre-test, various scenes appeared that could not be adequately described by one of the primary landscape types. Rather than roughly "pigeon-holing" the scene, it was decided that two primary types could be cited if the scene exhibited approximately equal attributes to the two compositional categories. Theoretically, one unusual overlook scene could be classified with two fundamental compositions and the two secondary types. During the process of classifying the slide library, no more than two primary and one secondary types were ever encountered.

Distance Zones. Distance of the observer from elements in the three-dimensional landscape is critical to how the viewer perceives the character of the visual display. A universally recognized axiom states that as sight-line distance increases, the visual significance of surface features (both in form and texture) decreases (Gibson, 1979). In response, visual resource managers have commonly divided the visible picture plane into three distinct distance zones derived from art definitions— foreground, midground, background. Boundaries separating these three zones in measurable distances have varied significantly between physiographic regions and individual researchers.

Although the Forest Service and the Bureau of Land Management have prescribed specific sight line distances for western landscapes, Felleman (1982) warns that significant differences between landform relief, vegetation types, and ambient atmospheric conditions make it inappropriate to apply these same standardized distances to forest environments in the eastern United States. Felleman proposes that in lieu of standardized distances, distance zone criteria be established for each regional area.

This suggestion is applicable to the Blue Ridge range, where dynamic fluctuations in atmospheric haze can play havoc with both perceived and real sight distances on a day-to-day basis. Under these conditions, we determined that standard measured distances were irrelevant. Rather, distinctions of visible clarity as indicated by standard elements in the landscape proved to be a more accurate approach to resolving the distance zone problem.

Litton (1968) and Bailey (1978) proposed descriptive characteristics specific to each of the distance zones. Foreground is defined as the part of the visual field containing the observer where maximum discernment of color, scale relationships, and landscape detail is possible. Midground is characterized mainly by the emergence of overall shapes and patterns in the landscape, visual discernment of the relationships between landscape units, the visual simplification of detail into texture, and the potential for aerial perspective. Background areas are classified as the sector of the picture plane where extreme visual simplification of landscape elements reveals only outlines of shapes, little to no texture, and color reduced to monochromatic hues distinguished by light and dark tones.

Armed with these criteria, we examined approximately 80 slides to establish concise, reliable, and replicable standards for determining distance zones. Being the predominate land cover of the Blue Ridge range, woody vegetation was initially identified as the one indicator. After repeated analysis, a recurring pattern developed in which the emergence of overall landscape patterns and vegetation texture coincided with that visual threshold at which individual leaves and branch complexes of vegetation were no longer discernable. Similarly, a second visual threshold was observed at the reduction of vegetation texture and the recognition of only landform outlines and tones of monochromatic colors. Consequently, the following definitions were established for each distance zone in this classification:

Foreground: The sector of the picture plane from the observer to the point at which individual leaves and/or vegetation branches were no longer discernable.

Midground: The section of the view from the point where individual leaves/branches are discernable to the point where texture in vegetation masses is no longer discernable.

Background: From the textural threshold to the horizon line.

Land Cover/Land Use Units

The land cover/land use unit continuum was developed directly from repeated examination of the slide library. Every type of man-made land use and natural land cover observed from the slides was recorded and then consolidated into the following classes:

Farm   —   all structures including barns, sheds, farmhouses, fences, livestock, mechanized equipment, and open spaces, whether in pasture, fallow, or cultivation, usually associated with agricultural activities. Gardens in the backyards of residential dwellings not associated with any of the above criteria were not included in this category.

Sparse Residential   —   all residential structures (single-family and two-family) and contiguous yard areas not associated with agricultural uses. Density of structures is limited to scattered development with no more than six units in close proximity to one another. Multi-family units were indiscernable from the slide library.

Town   —   all residential and non-residential structures exceeding the six-unit criteria in the sparse residential category. Land use patterns exhibited in the slide library appeared as either scattered single dwelling units or clustered hamlet development. The hamlet pattern was designated in this category. All roads, driveways, and visible sidewalks and paths with associated vegetation were also collapsed into this category. In most cases no more than four roadways were evident. Clustering usually occurred around one principal highway.

Town/Farm — similar to the land pattern exhibited in the town classification with the exception that agricultural uses were evident within and/or immediately surrounding the hamlet center.

Urban — high density residential and non-residential development, rectilinear layout of streets, more than four visible streets, and limited amounts of open space.

Transmission — high voltage transmission lines suspended from towers exceeding the height of residential utility poles; radio towers.

Mining — land subjected to either active or inactive strip-mining and quarrying procedures. All associated structures, processing equipment, utility service, and access roads were included in this category.

Transport — all highways and roads not directly associated with any previously defined category or the Blue Ridge Parkway; railroad lines and their appurtenant structures were included.

Deciduous Forest — all wildland forests not associated with human uses (such as windbreaks, street and yard trees, and buffers) and dominated by deciduous species.

Coniferous Forest — all wildland forests not associated with human land and dominated by coniferous species.

Mixed Forest — wildland forests not associated directly with human land uses and containing at least a 70%/30% mixture of both deciduous and coniferous species.

Clear-Cut — open space in forested stands where evidence exists that lumbering activities have occurred.

Stream/River	—	all observable watercourses in which photographic evidence suggests channelized water movement.
Pond/Wetland	—	all observable impounded water bodies and wetlands.
Escarpment	—	open space containing rock outcrops formed by natural geologic processes.
Information/ Recreation	—	all informational signs, recreational and informational structures (such as information booths, rest rooms, interpretative centers associated with developed recreational areas), open space developed for recreational activities including hiking and bicycle trails, picnic tables, etc.
Blue Ridge Parkway	—	incorporating both the pavement and mowed shoulders of the parkway.

Spatial Characteristics. As previously discussed, the unit modifiers were designed to identify those three-dimensional factors that characterize the land cover/land use units within the visual field. Ideally, these modifiers could include such dimensions as form, line, color, texture, scale, spatial enclosure, and edge definition. However, because of a variety of circumstances, it was either unnecessary or infeasible to consider all these factors in establishing the parameters of the modifiers.

Land cover in the Blue Ridge range is dominated by dense stands of mature, second-, and third-growth woody vegetation. As a result, non-forested land cover appears as open space carved out of the woodland carpet. Most of these non-forest land use/land covers appeared in the midground-background zones of the slides. Consequently, reduction of visual clarity and recognition resulting from distance and atmospheric effects made color, form, scale, and, to a degree, textural attributes considerably less distinguishable and, therefore, less of a factor in determination of landscape character. The configuration and complexity of open space and the edge definition at the forest/non-forest interface remained considerably clearer, and therefore, a more potent factor to characterizing the landscape.

Newby (1971) and other researchers seem to substantiate this observation. Edge definition is recognized as one of the principal sources in the landscape critical for spatial organization and information processing.

Based on our examination of scenes in the slide library, the following unit modifier categories were formulated:

Linear Space — the land cover is observed in the visual field to be aligned in a linear corridor. Originally, this modifier was further subdivided into linear and curvilinear categories. However, in the interest of maintaining a manageable set of variables, the two conditions were later collapsed into one category.

Geometric Space — land cover appearing in geometric form with angular edge definitions.

Organic Space — land cover assuming an organic configuration. Edges are not angular but predominated by arcs. Edges are fairly regular and not overly complex.

Digitate Space — land cover is essentially organic, yet edge is highly complex, punctuated by islands and peninsulas of forest protruding into the open space.

Dominant — the space occupied by the land cover/land use is dominant in the visual field and may be punctuated by other land covers of one of the preceding unit modifiers. For the most part, the forest seemed to exclusively occupy this category.

In rare situations in which forest was not the dominant land cover, the above categories still applied to the configuration and edge condition of the land.

Landform Series

The North Atlantic Regional Water Resources study (1972) identifies only two distinct topographic series for the Blue Ridge Mountains: (1) linear, rounded hills of varying height and (2) continuous linear ridges with occasionally scattered peaks. Derived from planimetric topographic maps, these descriptions do, indeed, summate the general, regional morphology of the range within the context of the eastern United States. However, within the context of the Blue Ridge Mountains, a broader spectrum of distinct landform types is encountered. The need for a more inclusive landform series is further substantiated by the fact that visual distortions produced by dramatic atmospheric effects and the observer's position within the three-dimensional landscape can present a perceived image of landform that differs significantly from the actual form of the terrain.

In an effort to develop a landform series applicable to the overlook scenes, the research team took the same approach that was used to formulate the land cover/land use units. The slide library was examined, and every perceivable landform type was inventoried. Over twenty categories were established. Upon pretest, it became evident that an unwieldly number of variables were being generated and a number of landform associations (especially certain valley-hill complexes) were recurring. The original 20 landform categories were collapsed into the following nine categories (see Figure 7.6):

Linear serrated ridgelines with conical peaks and intervening v-shaped valleys.

Undulating ridgelines with flanking lower, secondary conical peaks. Valley forms occupied a medial range between v-shaped and u-shaped.

Uniform ridgelines with rounded edges. No concave forms were associated, since these ridges were usually observed to be perpendicular to the overlook sight line. Thus, valleys were not visible because of interposing land forms.

Linear, steep, and rounded hills with u-shaped valleys. Often, these valleys were connected to broader flatlands.

Individual and linked, low rounded hills, usually associated with broad valleys.

Broad valleys with gentle, rolling floors.

Broad valleys with flat floors.

Side slopes—this series developed in response to the limited cone of vision inherent in the format of 35-mm photography. Often spurs from ridgelines, or the slope falling away from the overlook site would appear in the slide frame without revealing the nature of the parent landform.

Detailed landscapes—this category accommodated all scenes in which close-up views of signs, water courses, and forest pathways showed no discernable landform pattern.

Landform Orientation. The need for providing series modifiers arose from a recognition that the landform categories could provide a generic description of the basic form but failed to account for the manner in which these forms were arranged in three-dimensional space. Different arrangements and juxtapositions of landforms in relation to the viewer's sight line created different landform textures, spatial enclosure, and ridgeline vividness—hence, different landscape characteristics.

Our analysis proposed that the identification of landform orientation in relation to the observer would serve as the principal indicator in differentiating landform series arrangements. For example, undulating ridgelines parallel to the line of sight revealed interposed valleys. The scene would be marked by an accentuated spatial enclosure. In addition, the axial lines of parallel ridgetops and valley floors would lead the viewer's sight through the scene. Conversely, the same undulating ridges perpendicular to the sight line obstruct the view into interposed valleys, resulting in less evidence of enclosed space and the creation of strong horizon lines. Oblique landforms represent the median between parallel and perpendicular.

The landform modifiers defined for the classification system include (see Figure 7.7):

Perpendicular axis

Oblique axis

Perpendicular-descending axis

Oblique-descending axis

Parallel axis

Operation of the Classification System. The presence or absence of all elements in the final classification system was noted. We began the process by first determining the viewer position and the appropriate compositional type(s). Next, boundaries between the three distance zones were established. Beginning with the foreground of the picture plane, observations of land cover/land use units and corresponding modifiers and then the landform series and corresponding modifiers were checked off if present within the distance zone. This rating process was then replicated for the midground and background distance zones. Hypothetically, each overlook scene could contain 446 classification characteristics or variables.[1]

The binary rating approach served two basic purposes: (1) to minimize the opportunity for the researcher's personal biases to enter into the system and (2) to process a large slide sample in the shortest amount of time. By simply confining the range of the researcher's input to either "observed " or "not observed," the binary system offered a high degree of objectivity. In addition, definite boundaries between variables were established from the onset, thereby increasing the replicability and reliability of the system.

It should be noted that an alternative rating procedure was considered, in which the slides would be projected onto a uniform grid target,

---

[1]The number of variables in the classification system totaled 446. Although, hypothetically, all compositional types, land cover units and landform series variables could be observed in a single scene, only one viewer position was possible.

• Linear serrated ridgelines with conical peaks and intervening v-shaped valleys.

• Undulating ridgelines with flanking lower, secondary conical peaks. Valley forms occupied a medial range between v-shaped and u-shaped.

• Uniform ridgelines with rounded edges. No concave forms were associated, since these ridges were usually observed to be oriented perpendicular to the overlook sight line. Thus, valleys were not visible due to interposing land forms.

• Linear, steep and rounded hills with u-shaped valleys. Often, these valleys were connected to broader flatlands.

• Individual and linked, low rounded hills. Usually associated with broad valleys.

Figure 7.6.   Landform categories for the Blue Ridge Mountains.

- Broad valleys with gentle, rolling, floors.

- Broad valleys with flat floors.

- Side slopes—this series developed from response to the limited cone of vision inherent in the format of 35-mm photography. Often spurs from ridgelines, or the slope falling away from the overlook site would appear in the slide frame without revelation of the nature of the parent land form.

- Detailed landscapes—this category accommodated all scenes in which closeup views of signs, water courses and forest pathways showed no discernable land form pattern.

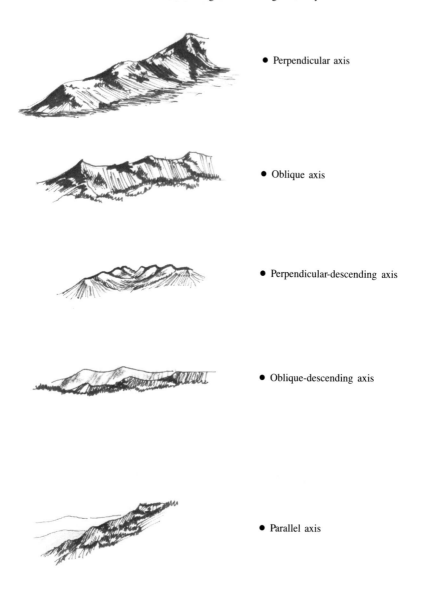

- Perpendicular axis

- Oblique axis

- Perpendicular-descending axis

- Oblique-descending axis

- Parallel axis

Figure 7.7.   Land form modifiers for the land form categories of the Blue Ridge Mountains.

and physical measurements of the landscape variables could be quantified. Although this alternative method would have provided a finer-grain dimension in the differentiation of landscape character, it was abandoned because of the prohibitive amount of time required to quantify 446 potential variables in a sample of 298 cases.

Classification of the Slide Library

Setup. Prior to the classification of each scene in the slide library, several setup procedures had to be completed. The slides (N = 298) were rearranged and numbered in the sequential order that a motorist, traveling south from the parkway entrance in Virginia, would encounter each overlook. Each slide was then assigned a copy of the classification form (see Figure 7.4) and labeled with the corresponding identification number.

Classification Procedures. Two researchers were each assigned the responsibility of classifying one-half of the slide library (including duplicates) using the binary rating system and criteria outlined previously. Upon completion of this task, the two researchers exchanged their classified forms and slides in order to check for reliability and replicability. In the few instances in which a rating disparity arose, the entire research team was assembled to arrive at a solution.

Discussion. As expected, unaccounted gray areas between certain variables did arise during the classification procedure—especially among the land cover/land use units. These problems occurred mostly in the mid-background in which distance and atmospheric effects obscured the land cover/land use character of open spaces. In such cases, dual modifiers were assigned (e.g., forest-dominant-digitate open space).

Although a statistical analysis was not conducted, the results of an interobserver reliability check seemed to show little variance between the ratings of the two researchers. This observation indicates that after a brief training period, the system affords a high degree of reliability and consistency. More extensive tests involving a larger sample of raters will be necessary to further substantiate the replicability of the classification method.

Comparison of Hammitt's Landscape Typology to Bio-Physical Classification

While our bio-physical landscape classification system attempted to keep track of multiple variables involved with viewer position (3), land cover/land use types (17), spatial characteristics (5), landform types (9), and landform orientations (5), Hammitt's system essentially broke the Blue Ridge Parkway into three sections and by factor analysis of viewer responses generated four major vista dimensions with each of the sections (see Table 7.2). Thus, Hammitt's system is not as much a landscape classification as a typology of major psychometric vista dimensions that may or may not relate to the many bio-physical factors previously listed. Clearly, many of the vista dimensions do relate to landform and vegetative and land use cover. It would clearly be desirable at some point to try to correlate bio-physical variables against psychometric vista dimensions to attempt to find significant relationships. By knowing these relationships, researchers and managers would know which environmental factors would be important to inventory or monitor for the optional management of the Blue Ridge Parkway.

Table 7.2. Hammitt's landscape sections and vista dimensions (from Chapter 2)

Northern Section
    Several-Ridged Vista
    Valley Development Vista
    Unmaintained Vista
    One-Ridged Vista
Middle Section
    Pond/Lake Vista
    Rolling Plateau Vista
    One-Ridged Vista
    Unmaintained Vista
Southern Section
    Stream/River Vista
    Farm Valley Vista
    Ridge and Valley Vista
    Unmaintained Vista

Selection of Images for Vegetative Management Simulations

Determining what slides (views) were suitable for simulation purposes was based largely on foreground vegetation. To simulate the results of possible vegetation management techniques, it was important to choose views (slides) that contained as much foreground plant material as possible. By using views that show vegetation from the ground to the crown (top), a more accurate simulation could be produced than by using views that just show the tops of plants. For example, if one vegetation management option showed controlled burning of shrubs, and the original view contained just the crowns of the plant material, then the simulation of burning would not portray the total effect of the burning. The effect on surrounding grasses and plants and the appearance of the ground could not be simulated.

Foreground Vegetation Suitability. The first phase in determining the suitability of foreground vegetation for simulation involved area measurements of all slides. The foreground vegetation in each slide was measured as a percentage of the entire scene. The slides were projected onto a grid. The number of grid sectors with foreground vegetation in them was then counted. If less than ⅓ of the sectors was filled with foreground vegetation, the view (slide) was eliminated from further consideration for simulation. The ⅓ rule was used for several reasons. First, if less than ⅓ of the slide showed foreground vegetation, the view could be overpowered by the emergent background scenery during a simulation of vegetation removal. The view might then be judged on the quality of the background and not on the management technique that was simulated. Second, to start eliminating some of the 298 slides from consideration, the ⅓ rule proved to be effective in reducing the number of possible slides for simulation to a manageable number. The slides that contained more than ⅓ foreground vegetation were then classified according to our foreground vegetation suitability index (Figure 7.8).

The foreground vegetation suitability index accomplished several things. It identified the amount of vegetation that could be seen from base to crown to crown alone in the primary and secondary vegetation (see Figure 7.8). It used a grid system to determine the dominant vegetation. The vegetation was then classified in order of dominance for easy reference and comparison of vegetation without viewing the grass as the dominant foreground vegetative feature, shrubs or shrub growth as secondary foreground vegetation, and mature deciduous trees as the third most dominant (see Figure 7.8).

As stated before, views that showed the vegetation from base to crown were determined to be the most applicable for simulation. The final phase for foreground vegetation suitability was the grouping of slides in two final categories. The first category included all the slides that had base to crown in both the primary and secondary foreground vegetation. This category was the most suitable for simulation according to foreground vegetation. The second category contained the slides with base to crown in either the primary or secondary foreground vegetation and base to mid-canopy in either or both the primary and secondary foreground vegetation. This category was marginal for simulation. In the final analysis, 10 slides were determined suitable for simulation according to foreground vegetation, and 21 slides (views) were marginal.

Frequency Analysis for Representation of Visual Elements. Using the Statistical Analysis System (SAS) computer program, frequencies were calculated for all 298 views and for the 10 slides used for simulations.

SLIDE NUMBER_____

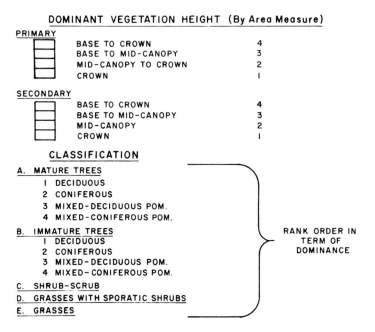

Figure 7.8.   Foreground vegetation suitability index.

The frequency tabulations provide an analysis of the individual elements incorporated in each composition determined through the classification matrix.

Under the landscape classification system (Figure 7.4), 443 possible elements existed for the make-up of each composition. There was the possibility of eight compositional types; 255 possibilities existed through the combination of three distance zones, five form modifiers, and 17 land uses; 180 possibilities existed through the combination of three distance zones, five series modifiers, 10 landscape series, and finally three viewer positions. Frequency analysis provided the number of observations for each element (the number of times an element was used) and the frequency for that element (the percentage of times the element was used to the number of total observations, 288 or 10). For example, out of the total 298 slide library, there was a total of 86 slides with a panoramic composition, for a frequency of 29.8%. This indicated to us that three (or 30%) of the final 10 slides used for simulation should also have a panoramic composition. Actually only one slide out of the 10 (10%) had a panoramic composition. From the results of the foreground vegetation suitability index, we only had 10 suitable slides to work with; if a certain element was missing, we had no way to substitute for it. We also had no way of determining if the original 298 slides showed an accurate representation of the views from all the scenic overlooks along the Blue Ridge Parkway. Without this knowledge we could not be sure that our simulations were an accurate representation. We did know that views from the majority of overlooks were photographed, but we did not know if the views were fully representive. Therefore, we needed the frequency analysis as a means to determine what, if any, elements were not represented in the simulation photos.

Out of the possible 443 elements, 99 were used to make up the composition of the original 298 slides, and 31 of those were used in the final 10 simulations. Therefore, 68 elements were not represented in the simulation photos. Of these, only five with an original frequency of 10% or more were not represented. They are: (1) organic green open space in the midground (which had a frequency of 12.4% out of the 298 original slides), (2) linear transportation in the midground (14.4%); (3) organic deciduous forest in the foreground (12%); (4) perpendicular rolling broad valley in the midground (10%); and (5) perpendicular linear serrated mountains in the background (23.3%). Out of these, transportation, rolling broad valleys, and linear serrated mountains were the only elements over 10% which were not represented one way or another in the simulations. Green open spaces were represented in the simulation seven times with different form modifiers or distance zones, and deciduous forests were represented 16 different times but not in an organic form in the foreground. The frequency counts show that a majority of elements (73.2%) that were above 10% were represented in the simulation; the counts also indicate those elements that showed up the most. Additional statistics are available in Table 7.3.

Having laid the groundwork in this chapter for selecting scenes to be included in the photo simulation, the next chapter deals with the techniques of the photo simulation process.

Table 7.3. Landscape classification percentages.

COMPOSITIONAL TYPES	TOTAL		SIMULATION	
	N	%	N	%
PANORAMA	86	28.9	1	10
FEATURE	60	20.1	5	50
ENCLOSED	112	37.6	6	60
FOCAL	55	18.4	3	30
CANOPIED	22	8.4	1	10
EPHEMERAL	136	46.3	4	40
DETAILED	7	2.3	—	—
OTHER	16	5.4	—	—
DISTANCE ZONES				
INFERIOR	46	15.4	2	20
NORMAL	180	43.6	5	50
SUPERIOR	118	39.6	3	30
LAND USE				

SYMBOLS TO INTERPRET LAND USE:
F = FOREGROUND, M = MIDGROUND, B = BACKGROUND
1 = LINEAR, 2 = ORGANIC, 3 = GEOMETRIC, 4 = DIGITATE, 5 = DOMINANT

GREEN OPEN SPACE				
FG01	10	3.4	2	20
FG02	5	1.7	2	20
FGO5	9	3.0	1	10
MG03	9	3.0	1	10
BG02	26	8.7	1	10
MG01	10	3.4	—	—
MG02	37	12.4	—	—
MG04	16	5.4	—	—
MG05	1	0.3	—	—
BG01	9	3.0	—	—
MG03	4	1.3	—	—
FARM				
FFA2	1	0.3	1	10
MFA2	13	4.4	2	20
BFA2	2	0.7	1	10
MFA3	8	2.7	—	—
SPARSE RESIDENTIAL				
MRE1	14	4.7	2	20
MRE2	9	3.0	1	10
RES. TOWN				
MRT3	1	0.3	1	10
URBAN				
BUR3	1	0.3	1	10
TRANSMISSION				
MTR1	8	2.4	1	10

Table 7.3 (cont'd).

COMPOSITIONAL TYPES	TOTAL		SIMULATION	
	N	%	N	%
DECIDUOUS FOREST				
FFD1	82	27.5	5	50
FFD5	32	10.7	2	20
MFD5	159	53.4	12	120
BFD5	196	65.8	19	190
MFD1	14	4.7	5	50
FFD2	36	12.0	—	—
MIXED FOREST				
FFM2	11	3.7	1	10
FFM5	15	5.0	3	30
MFM5	69	23.2	7	70
FFM3	1	0.3	1	10
MFM2	5	1.7	2	20
BFM2	1	0.3	1	10
FFM1	15	5.0	—	—
BFM5	14	4.7	—	—
CLEAR CUT				
MCC3	3	1.0	1	10
BCC2	12	4.0	—	—
BCC4	2	0.7	—	—
STREAM/RIVER				
FSR1	6	2.0	—	—
ESCARP/MINING				
MEM2	12	4.0	1	10
MEM4	10	3.4	1	10
INFO/RECREATION				
FIR1	1	0.3	1	10
FIR3	1	0.3	—	—
FIR5	5	1.7	—	—
PARKWAY/R.O.W.				
FBR1	6	2.0	2	20
FBR3	1	0.3	—	—
FBR5	1	0.3	—	—

LANDSCAPE SERIES
F = FOREGROUND, M = MIDGROUND, B = BACKGROUND
1 = PERPENDICULAR, 2 = OBLIQUE HORZ., 3 = OBLIQUE DECEND.,
4 = DECEND, 5 = PARALLEL

BROAD ROLLING				
VALLEY				
FVR1	2	0.7	—	—
FVR3	1	0.3	—	—
MVR1	30	10.0	—	—
MVR3	6	2.0	—	—
FLAT BROAD VALLEY				
BVF1	12	4.0	1	10
FVF1	2	0.7	—	—
MVF3	2	0.7	—	—

Table 7.3 (cont'd).

COMPOSITIONAL TYPES	TOTAL		SIMULATION	
	N	%	N	%
DETAILED				
FDE1	8	2.7	1	10
FDE3	1	0.3	—	—
FDE5	7	2.3	—	—
MDE3	1	0.3	—	—
ISOLATED CONICAL PEAKS				
BCP1	21	7.0	2	20
BCP1	10	3.4	—	—
LOW HILLS LINKED				
MCH1	9	3.0	—	—
LINEAR SERRATED				
BLS1	69	23.2	—	—
MLS4	5	1.7	—	—
ISOLATED LOW HILLS				
MHI1	15	5.0	1	10
BHI1	5	1.7	—	—
SIDESLOPE				
MSS1	9	3.0	1	10
FSS3	2	0.7	—	—
FSS5	1	0.3	—	—
MSS2	10	3.4	—	—
MSS4	6	2.0	—	—
UNDULAT. RIDGE				
MDR1	41	13.8	4	40
BDR1	107	35.9	4	40
MDR2	7	2.3	—	—
MDR3	12	4.0	—	—
MDR5	11	3.7	—	—
BDR3	10	3.4	—	—
UNDULAT. RIDGE/VALLEY				
MER1	16	5.4	—	—
BER1	3	1.0	—	—
MER3	13	4.4	—	—
MER4	12	4.0	—	—
MER5	16	5.4	—	—
LINEAR HILLS				
MLH3	5	1.7	1	10
MLH4	3	1.0	1	10
BLH1	4	1.3	—	—
MLH1	12	4.0	—	—
UNIFORM RIDGES				
BFR1	23	7.7	1	10
MFR2	4	1.3	1	10
MFR1	9	3.0	—	—
BFR4	1	0.3	—	—

REFERENCES

Anderson, P.F. 1979. Analysis of landscape character for visual resource management. *In* G.H. Elsner and R.C. Smardon (Tech. Coord.), *Our National Landscape*.

Baker, W.A. 1972. *The Blue Ridge*. New York, New York: Viking Press.

Bailey, R.G. 1978. *Description of the Eco-Regions of the United States*. Washington, D.C.: U.S. Department of Agriculture, Forest Service.

Bittenger, L.F. 1901 (republished 1968). *The Germans in Colonial Times*. New York, New York: Russel and Russel.

Bolton, C.K. 1967. *Scotch-Irish Pioneers in Ulster and America*. Baltimore, Maryland: Geneological Publishing Co.

Elsner, G.H., and R. C. Smardon. (Tech. Coord.). 1979. Our national landscape: proceedings of a conference on applied techniques for analysis and management of the visual resource. Incline Village, Nevada, April 23–25, 1979. USDA Forest Service Gen. Tech. Rpt. PSW-35, Pacific Southwest Forest and Range Experiment Station, Berkeley, California.

Felleman, J.P. 1979. *Landscape Visibility—Theory and Practice*. Syracuse, New York: School of Landscape Architecture, State University of New York.

Felleman, J.P. 1982. Visibility mapping in New York's Coastal Zone: A case study of alternative methods. *Coastal Zone Management Journal* 9: 249–270.

Ford, H.J. 1966. *The Scotch-Irish in America*. Camden, Connecticut: Archon Books.

Gibson, J.J. 1979. *The Ecological Approach to Visual Perception*. Boston, Massachusetts: Houghton Mifflin.

Graeff, A.D., et al. 1942. *The Pennsylvania Germans*. Princeton, New Jersey: Princeton University Press.

Jolley, H. 1969. *The Blue Ridge Parkway*. Knoxville, Tennessee: University of Tennessee.

Kercheval, S. 1902. *History of the Valley of Virginia*. Woodstock, Virginia: W.N. Grabill.

Kollmorgen, W.M. 1942. The Pennsylvania German Farmer. *In* A.D. Graeff et al. *The Pennsylvania Germans*. Princeton, New Jersey: Princeton University Press.

Litton, R.B., Jr. 1968. Forest landscape description and inventories: a basis for land planning and design. USDA Forest Service Research Paper PSW-49, Pacific Southwest Forest and Range Experiment Station, Berkeley, California.

Long, A., Jr. 1972. *The Pennsylvania German Family Farm*. Publications of the Pennsylvania German Society, Vol. 6. Breings, Pennsylvania: The Pennsylvania German Society.

Mitchell, E. 1835. Notice of height of mountains in North Carolina. *American Journal of Science and Arts* 35: 378p.

Newby, F.L. 1971. Understanding the visual resource. *In Forest Recreation Synposium*. Northeast Forest Recreation Experiment Station. Upper Darby, Pennsylvania. 68–72pp.

North Atlantic Regional Water Resources Study Coordinating Committee. 1972. Appendix N: Visual and Cultural Environment. Prepared by Research Planning and Design Associates, Inc. for North Atlantic Regional Water Resources Study Coordinating Committee, New York, New York.

Opie, J. 1981. Where American history began: Appalachia and the small independent family farm. *In* W. Somerville (Ed.), *Appalachia/America. Proceedings of the Appalachian Studies Conference*, Boone, TN. East Tennessee State University, The Appalachian Consortium Press.

Palmer, J.F. 1983. An investigation of the conceptual classification of landscapes and its application to landscape planning issues. *In* S. Weidemann & J.R. Anderson (Eds.), *Priorities for Environmental Design Research, Part I*. Washington, D.C.: Environmental Design Research Association.

Palmer, J.F. 1983. Assessing coastal wetlands in Dennis, Massachusetts. *In* R.C. Smardon (Ed.), *The Future of Wetlands: Assessing Visual-Cultural Values*. Totowa, New Jersey: Allenheld-Osmun Co.

Riddel, F.S. (Ed.). 1974. *Appalachia: Its People, Heritage, and Problems*. Dubuque, Iowa: Kendall/Hunt Publishing Co.

Sheppard, M.E. 1935. *Cabins in the Laurel*. Chapel Hill, North Carolina: University of North Carolina Press.

Simpkins, O.N. 1974. The celtic roots of Appalachian culture. *In* F.S. Riddel (Ed.), *Appalachia: Its People, Heritage and Problems*. Dubuque, Iowa: Kendall/Hunt Publishing Co.

Smardon, R.C., and T. Mahon. 1980. Forests in the visual landscape. *Resource Planning Assessment Report No. 14*, N.Y. State Department of Environmental Conservation, Bureau of Forests and Resource Management, Albany, New York.

Smathers, G. A. 1982. *Man as a Factor in the Southern Appalachians: Bald Formation and Illustrations of Selected Sites along the Blue Ridge Parkway in North Carolina*. U.S. Department of Interior, National Park Service.

Stilgoe, J.R. 1982. *Common Landscape of America: 1580 to 1845*. New Haven, Connecticut: Yale University Press.

U.S. Department of Agriculture, Forest Service. 1973. National Forest Land-scape Management System, Vol. 1, USDA Handbook. United States Government Printing Office, Publication No. 0100–2583, Washington, D.C.

Weller, J. E. 1965. *Yesterday's People: Life in Contemporary Appalachia.* Frankfort, Kentucky: University Press of Kentucky.

Wells. B. 1937. Southern Appalachian grass balds. *Journal of Elisha Mitchell Science Society* 53(1): 1–26.

Zeisel, J. 1981. *Inquiry by Design: Tools for Environment-Behavior Research.* Monterey, California: Brooks/Cole Publishing Co.

Chapter Eight
Simulating and Evaluating Management Practices

James F. Palmer, Timothy R. Day, Richard C. Smardon,
Tad Redway, and Lawrence Reichardt
State University of New York
Syracuse, New York

This chapter reports on two further contributions of the State University of New York (SUNY) College of Environmental Science and Forestry to the Blue Ridge Parkway study. First, National Park Service (NPS) personnel were shown how to prescribe actual vegetation management practices for particular vistas. These management prescriptions were then translated into visual simulations. The visual simulations were incorporated into a questionnaire and distributed to respondents, as detailed in previous chapters and in Appendix B. Second, an independent statistical analysis of the responses to this questionnaire was conducted. These reactions were then interpreted for management purposes. Finally, the results of the historic analysis presented in Chapter 7 and a psychometric analysis of the data are combined into a set of recommendations for vegetative management near scenic vistas along the Blue Ridge Parkway.

Vegetative Management Simulations

Introduction to Simulation Procedures
This section describes the simulation procedures used for a viewer survey in which certain vegetation management techniques used by the National Park Service were simulated for the Blue Ridge Parkway.

Many techniques are currently being used to simulate landscape change, ranging from sketches to computer-generated imagery. In this case, we used the technique of photographic montage, wherein photographs are altered by cutting out and pasting in new visual information.

Before any technique is used to demonstrate or predict vegetative modification, several critical questions should be addressed (Sheppard, 1982). How much realism is required? Can the change or proposed idea be sketched? Should the photography be in black and white or color? Is the budget adequate to meet the need?

Several techniques in photomontage are described in the Visual Resource Management (VRM) Manual published by the Bureau of Land Management (USDI, Bureau of Land Management, 1980) and in a paper presented by Stephen Sheppard (1979) at the Bureau of Land Management Computer Graphic Conference. While we found these descriptions helpful in deciding what technique to use, no examples in the literature describe a purely vegetal form of change such as the one encountered in the Blue Ridge Parkway Study. Sheppard's notes cover all of the two-and three-dimensional elements. However, there are no specifics related solely to vegetal materials.

Basically, change to the landscape involves four components: landform, vegetation, water bodies, and structures. Change may involve adding elements, subtracting elements, or both. The problems encountered in this project involved the selective addition and deletion of vegetation in the foreground of highly complex vegetated scenes. Thus, the problems were, perhaps, more difficult than the examples presented in the VRM Manual and will be discussed here in detail.

Simulation Process

Response Format/Visual Display. The first problem we addressed was the final product, because all other decisions depended on it. For this project the final product was determined to be standard $8'' \times 10''$ color photographs for ease in handling.

The next step was to determine the images that would be required to produce the final product. Two factors were of prime concern: (1) the visual impact of roadside vegetation on the Blue Ridge Parkway visitor and (2) the impact of management techniques utilized by the Park Service along the parkway.

Data Treatment. The 298 color slides taken along the parkway by University of Tennessee investigators were coded and classified (as previously described in Chapter 7) to determine representative scenes from parkway overlooks. The next step was to apply appropriate management techniques to each scene. To accomplish this task, advice from Park Service managers was sought.

Each of the 10 representative scenes was printed, inserted into an acetate envelope, and sent, together with an acetate marker, to the Blue Ridge Parkway maintenance supervisor in Asheville, North Carolina. Comments and graphic delineations from the Park Service managers were drawn directly on the acetate overlays and returned. The managers identified three major management techniques common to the 10 representative scenes: first, mowing either by bush hog on accessible sites or by hand cutting; second, selective cutting of brush or trees to allow for significant views; and third, controlled burning in places inaccessible to machines (Figure 8.1).

To conduct the simulation, three pieces of information were obtained: United States Geological Survey (USGS) quadrangle maps for background topographical data, photographs taken from behind the vegetation to be removed or modified, and photographs snapped in front of the scene for contextual information. Photographs taken from behind vegetation are crucial because the three management techniques supplied by the Park Service involved eliminating vegetation by one means or another, which would reveal new vegetation, topography, or manmade form.

Another concern we addressed was seasonal variation. Some management techniques might have a significant impact on views in summer, but the impact on views in winter might be quite different. Possible procedures might be to consider proposed changes with different seasonal impacts or to choose the season with the highest visitation frequency, such as summer with vegetation in full leaf. In this case the latter procedure was used. It is important that simulations be made for the same season in which subjects will be responding to a photo questionnaire.

Specific Visual Simulation Techniques

Prototypical Scene Development. As stated before, the purpose of the project was to solicit visitor responses to certain NPS vegetation management techniques. After the representative scenes were chosen and comments were received from the National Park Service (summarized in Figure 8.1), each scene was analyzed to determine the appropriate montage technique. This was accomplished by overlaying the original 8" x 10" print with acetate and registering them with the USGS quadrangles to determine hidden topographic features. Ideas were tested using markers, as illustrated in Figure 8.2.

After the appropriate montage technique was selected and done, the 8" × 10" finished photomontages were photographically reduced to 2" × 3" size for inclusion in the questionnaire (Appendix B) . Three pages with six images per page were prepared. Each page contained the

SUNSET FIELD 78.4 Mile Post

Existing view is very good. But some improvement of near foreground could be done by controlled burning.

BOBLETS GAP 93.1 Mile Post

Existing view is excellent.
(1) The area in the near foreground should be hand cut.
(2) The area in the immediate foreground should be a part of the mowing plan.

MT. HARDY 422.8 Mile Post

Existing view is good. An opportunity exists to emphasize spruce species at this area. To do this cutting hardwoods would be necessary.

MOSES CONE 293.5 Mile Post

Existing view is average. A need for thinning is necessary to open up view. Selective cutting would be recommended.

Figure 8.1.   Examples of major management techniques represented in vista scenes.

before and after images of our scenes, and each photograph had a brief caption and rating scale beneath it. Consequently, the respondents were able to compare the before and after photos of each scene and give us their ratings of the various vegetation management techniques.

The following sections describe the materials and methods we employed during the course of our photographic montage work, the problems we encountered, and the techniques and materials we found most suitable for meeting our purposes. Use of trade names does not imply endorsement of commercial products by either the U.S. Government or the State University of New York.

ROANOKE BASIN 112.9 Mile Post

No specific need for vegetative management is indicated at this point. However, the grass bay areas of the immediate foreground could trim the view. A wide range of textures becomes complimentary in such urban views.

LANE PINNACLE 372.1 Mile Post

Here the vegetation in the near foreground is not obstructing to the distant view, so it may be left alone at this time. The grass in the immediate foreground should be in the mowing plan.

WHITE'S GAP 44.4 Mile Post

This framing view is average.
(1) Selective cutting should be done in near foreground to open framing view to mountains.
(2) Immediate foreground should be cleared by handwork or controlled burning.

Figure 8.2.   Acetate overlays on 8 in. × 10 in. photos were used to determine the appropriate montage technique to be used.

Products and Processing Attributes and Constraints. The Image Library, furnished by University of Tennessee researchers for this project, consisted of slides, so we used manufactured products that were designed to produce direct prints without reshooting. The three products we used included Ilford's Cibachrome processing (Ilford, 1974; and Ilford, undated) for color prints on glossy paper, which has a synthetic composition backing; Cibachrome in a matte finish with a paper backing; and Kodak's Ekta-Print processing (Eastman Kodak, 1981 and 1982). Time, equipment availability, and familiarity with these products influenced the decision of which product to use. Each product, how-

NORTH COVE 327.3 Mile Post

Existing view is pretty good. The middle foreground should be cleared by selective cutting. This would open near ridgeline to left in view. The immediate foreground should be cleared by handwork or controlled burning.

BOSTON KNOB 38.8 Mile Post

Nothing practical can be done to improve this view at this vantage point. At this geological scale vegetative management can only be done by cooperative agreement with the U.S. Forest Service.

SHEETS GAP 252.7 Mile Post

The existing view is average. At this vantage point the large oak on right becomes a frame.
(1) In near foreground selective cutting is needed to open view to left.
(2) The area in the immediate foreground should be a part of the mowing plan.

Figure 8.2   (cont.)

ever, contains different properties relevant to most montaging techniques.

While camera-ready graphics dictate that photographs be glossy to obtain the highest resolution possible, the Cibachrome's glossy synthetic backing presented a problem. To avoid undesirable white edges in a "cut and paste" image application, we found it necessary to strip the backing from the emulsion layers. The Cibachrome glossy is difficult, if not impossible, to strip. Another limitation of the Cibachrome glossy is that fingerprints are difficult to remove after much handling.

The Ekta-Print processing promised to be advantageous in terms of development time, but image quality and exposure latitude proved to be major limiting factors. Thus, because of the limitations of these two products for our purposes, it was decided to use Cibachrome's matte finish material, which provided adequate image quality and exposure latitude and allowed for stripping the backing.

Because we were already set up for printing from slides, the 8" × 10" simulations were rephotographed onto slides and printed at the required 2" × 3" camera-ready size. The slides were printed on Polaroid's 690 print paper using a Vivitar slide copier since this print size was very close to the final product size desired.

Simulation Development Techniques. Several methods and media were used to develop the simulations. The first and most commonly used technique was "cut and paste." Depending on the amount of change required, two approaches were used. First, in relatively small areas—for example, a bank of large shrubs that needed to be eliminated and replaced with smaller shrubs or grass while providing appropriate background material—a technique called "windowing" was performed (Figure 8.3). This involved cutting out the material to be changed, stripping the backing ¼ in. or so from the hole, appling cement to edges, and registering and applying the new material to the back.

When relatively large areas of the image, such as a tree mass, mountains, or sky, needed to be altered, a technique we called "layering" was used (Figure 8.4). Again, we simply trimmed away the material to be changed, stripped the backing from the edge to be retained, and cemented new material in place.

The next most common technique we used was called "coloring." In our project, use of coloring was confined to "touch-up." Surprisingly, the "marker" variety of color application proved quite successful for sky and mountain touch-up, but only in small areas where the usual "blobbing" problem with markers can be discreetly hidden behind black or dark areas. We also tried color pencils to blend existing and new vegetation but without significant results. However, in some in-

WINDOWING

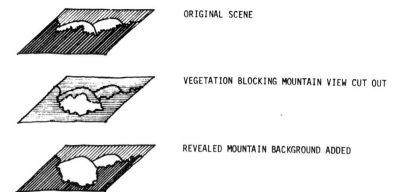

ORIGINAL SCENE

VEGETATION BLOCKING MOUNTAIN VIEW CUT OUT

REVEALED MOUNTAIN BACKGROUND ADDED

Figure 8.3.   Demonstration of the "windowing" technique to remove small areas of vegetation from a vista scene.

LAYERING

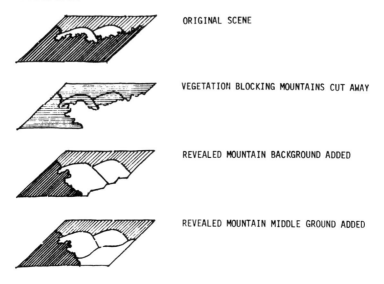

ORIGINAL SCENE

VEGETATION BLOCKING MOUNTAINS CUT AWAY

REVEALED MOUNTAIN BACKGROUND ADDED

REVEALED MOUNTAIN MIDDLE GROUND ADDED

Figure 8.4.   Demonstration of the "layering" technique to remove relatively large areas of vegetation from a vista scene.

stances the pencils worked quite well in adding texture and shadow to background mountains.

Color dyes matched to the Cibachrome print material seemed to work best for touch-up in most instances (Ilford, 1983; and Ilford, undated). The kit, manufactured by Cibachrome, is essentially a water-based activated dye that penetrates the emulsion layers of the print material when applied by brush. The primary advantage of the dyes over the markers is the control over the amount of color placed in contact with the print through the use of a fine-tipped artist's brush. The dyes are particularly well suited for vegetation where textural addition is needed to mask splices, and since dyes are water-soluble, a mistake can be corrected by simply washing off. The dyes seemed to work equally well on the Polaroid and Cibachrome material.

Discussion

Perhaps the most basic problem in our photomontage project was that of obtaining new vegetation material. Whenever possible, we used material from a second print of the scene and rearranged it to suit the goal of the simulation. It was very difficult to exactly match the texture and color of material taken from a different scene.

During field reconnaissance, photographs of vegetation surrounding the view in areas with similar viewing positions and lighting were taken so that materials seen from an appropriate distance were available for matching when needed.

Related to this problem was the issue of perspective. All scenes we dealt with were views taken from ridge tops with slopes falling rapidly away from the viewer position. Whenever material was taken from a different scene, it was crucial to match the topography as closely as possible.

Finally, while many yardsticks can be used to measure the success of any project, one that might be applied here is the ease with which the process might be duplicated. Simulation projects such as this one have traditionally fallen to highly skilled artists, often with very sophisticated technology. The attempt here was to produce high quality simulations using average skills, methods, and technology commonly found in professional offices or schools with access to darkroom facilities.

Visual Preference Evaluations

The ratings of how much the respondents liked the simulated effects of management alternatives are summarized in Table 8.1. The sites have been grouped according to the general management practice they represent. The mean values ($\bar{x}$) represent the difference between the ratings for the less managed or control condition and the more managed or treatment condition. Therefore, a negative value represents visual improvement and a value of zero indicates no change in visual quality. A t-test was used to identify those cases where the mean change is significantly different from zero. The mean differences and t-tests are reported for those who received the information leaflet and those who did not. A paired comparison t-test was used to identify significant differences between the mean change in ratings for these two groups.

In addition, an analysis of variance model (reported in Table 8.2) was used to investigate the effects of these factors. Among the effects incorporated into these models is "activity," or the significance of the change in rating from the control (photo a) to the treatment (photo b) condition. The "information" effect refers to the difference between those who did and did not receive the interpretive message (see Becker, et al., Chapter 6). In a sense, each of the simulated sites is a repeated measure of a particular management activity. Collectively, they repre-

Table 8.1. Mean change in visual preference ratings for simulated management situations.

Condition	Site	With Leaflet $\bar{x}^1$	t	Without Leaflet $\bar{x}$	t	Paired-t
Mowing width	1	1.57	10.4***	1.72	11.7***	−.7 n.s.
	2	1.32	9.0***	.95	5.9***	1.7 n.s.
	3	.21	1.2 n.s.	−.29	−1.7 n.s.	2.1*
	6	1.03	6.4***	.47	2.7**	2.4*
	7	−1.50	−10.1***	−1.19	−7.3***	−1.4 n.s.
	9	1.00	5.8***	.64	3.4***	1.4 n.s.
Mowing frequency	8	.13	.8 n.s.	−.45	−3.0***	2.6**
Sign mowing	4	−1.71	−10.7***	−2.36	−18.1***	3.1**
Major clearing	10	−1.89	−14.5***	−2.13	−17.7***	1.4 n.s.
	12	−.30	−1.8 n.s.	−.16	−1.0 n.s.	−.6 n.s.
	13	−.06	−.4 n.s.	−.23	−1.3 n.s.	.7 n.s.
	16	−2.57	−23.4**	−2.55	−24.7***	−.1 n.s.
Moderate clearing	11	−.32	2.1*	−.31	−1.9 n.s.	−.1 n.s.
	14	1.53	11.2***	1.36	9.8***	.9 n.s.
	17	1.35	9.6***	1.18	7.9***	.8 n.s.
	18	.35	2.5*	.25	1.7 n.s.	.5 n.s.
Controlled burning	5	1.35	9.1***	1.19	7.7***	.8 n.s.
	15	−.19	−1.1 n.s.	−.17	−1.0 n.s.	−.1 n.s.

***p< .001   **p< .01   *p< .05   n.s. denotes p≥ .05

[1] The mean difference is a less managed or control condition rating, minus a more managed or treatment condition. Negative values indicate visual improvement.

sent the visual variation of using these practices in the landscape. This variation is represented by a "site" effect. For the analysis of vista clearing, a second model grouped the sites into clearing activities of major and moderate intensity. All possible two-way interactions were also included in these models.

The pattern of visual preference for mowing alternatives is very similar between the two groups. Overall, respondents preferred the control or less mown condition. The major exception was a preference for mowing vegetation around a low road sign (site 8). The treatment in

Table 8.2. Effects of management activity, information and site ratings of visual preference.[1]

Management Action	Effects	df	F-value
Mowing width	Activity	1	595.4***
	Information	1	6.2*
	Site	5	10.1***
	Info + Activity	1	23.5***
	Info + Site	5	.4 n.s.
	Activity + Site	5	40.5***
Controlled burning	Activity	1	69.6***
	Information	1	.2 n.s.
	Site	1	2.4 n.s.
	Info + Activity	1	.5 n.s.
	Info + Site	1	.1 n.s.
	Activity + Site	1	140.8***
Vista clearing between sites	Activity	1	92.8***
	Information	1	.1 n.s.
	Site	7	13.2**
	Info + Activity	1	1.2 n.s.
	Info + Site	7	.2 n.s.
	Activity + Site	7	295.5***
Vista clearing by major and moderate treatments	Activity	1	81.9***
	Information	1	.1 n.s.
	Intensity	1	46.3***
	Info + Activity	1	1.1 n.s.
	Info + Intensity	1	.3 n.s.
	Activity + Intensity	1	969.7***

***$p < .001$ **$p < .01$ *$p < .05$ n.s. denotes $p \geq .05$

[1] Among the effects incorporated into the analysis of variance models, activity refers to control (photo a) and treatment (photo b) conditions. Information refers to those who did or did not receive the information leaflet. Site refers to those sites simulating the activity; in a sense these are simulation repetitions or repeated measures of the management activity. Intensity regroups the vista clearing sites into major and moderate clearings. The two-way interactions are also indicated.

site 7 also received a very positive rating. However, this may be because the two photographs were of distinctly different sites.

Significant differences were found between the mean change for these two groups at half the sites, which is similar to the influence among the mowing management statements. This result was supported by a significant effect in the analysis of variance model for mowing width, as well as the t-tests for mowing frequency (site 8) and mowing around road signs (site 4). In all these analyses, the interpretive message was associated with preference for reduced mowing activity. This effect was accentuated among those who received the message, accounting for the significant interactive term (Becker, et al. Chapter 6).

The most significant effect in the analysis of variance model for mowing width concerns the change at each site from a more intensive management practice. As has already been described, respondents generally support less intensive mowing. The actual variation among the sites was also highly significant, possibly indicating the relative difference in treatment intensity between photos at a particular site as well as the visual sensitivity of different sites to management practices. The significant interaction between activity and site was attributable to the essential lack of difference between the photographs at site 3.

The overall preference for the visual effects of vista management practices is clearer, though different, than it was for mowing practices. Cutting activity that removes large amounts of woody vegetation from an overgrown vista to establish an open view was preferred. However, the respondents did not appear to support cutting when the vista was only slightly blocked or when a significant area of residual vegetation is left that still blocked the view. This result seems to support responses to the management statements, where cutting was supported every 5 to 7 years (seemingly a long time) over annual clearing or clearing before one-third of the view is blocked. Controlled burning also received poor ratings, particularly in the case where there was little change in the vista's extent. Finally, there were no significant differences between the two groups, indicating that the interpretive message had no effect. This may be because the message focused on mowing, and the effect failed to carry over to tree clearing. Alternately, it may be because respondents already had a clear position on vista management that is based on a cultural reticence to cut down trees but a strong visual preference for vistas.

These findings are supported by the analysis of variance results. The actual change in evaluation from the pre- to post-activity was highly significant. In addition, when they were collapsed into major and moderate intensity groups, the results were again highly significant. We also found a highly significant interaction effect between the activity and site or intensity factors. Essentially, this represents a strong preference for major clearings and a perceived undesirability of only modest clearings. The controlled burning analysis exhibited a similar pattern for activity and the interactive term.

Summary and Management Recommendations

Bio-Physical and Historical Management Recommendations

Any vegetative management technique should be preceded by a thorough analysis of the goals and objectives to be accomplished. Since the primary object of this research involved the human cultural aspect of viewing from the Blue Ridge Parkway, a number of physical parameters should be considered. Basically, viewing from the Blue Ridge Parkway involves two major components: the position of the viewer and the scene to be viewed. Viewer position generally refers to either viewing at a scenic overlook while standing or sitting, or viewing along the road while in a moving car. The speed of the car and the road configuration are also important because an impressive view is more likely to be seen while on a straight road at a low speed than on a curve except by a passenger. The amount of vegetation to be removed should be determined not only by what is viewed but whether the viewer is moving or standing still.

The major management constraint on the scene to be viewed is not only the vegetation, but also the underlying topography. Most of the Blue Ridge Parkway is located along relatively steep slopes or on ridge tops. This means the major long views contain foregrounds that slope away from the viewer. The management techniques utilized—controlled burning and cutting or mowing—are effective especially in preventing severe erosion on steep slopes and in soils that are largely thin, well-drained, and of low fertility. However, because the climate is highly conducive to plant growth, sites of prime viewing require constant care. Basically, any native plant material considered for revegetative purposes should be self-maintaining and physically and micro-climatically appropriate to the area and the surrounding vegetal context of the view and the slope on which it is placed.

Environmentally, any plantings of native perennial vegetation should use those species that contain certain characteristics. First, since most soils on steep slopes and ridges are thin and low in nutrients, the plants should be shallow and fibrous-rooted and have the ability to absorb and hold nutrients for extended periods of time. Second, since the climate is humid and temperate and the rainfall is abundant, the plants should be able to withstand the potential erosive effects of heavy rainfall, snow, and sedimentation.

Physically, any native plants selected for revegetation should be complementary in terms of form, size, and texture to the surrounding site context. Even more importantly, the height of the plants should be self-maintaining and predictable, since placement on a given slope with respect to the viewer position is crucial in maintaining the desired view. Native grasses such as broomsedge could be used in near foreground areas, but if the slope falls away sharply, native shrubs could be used. Again, consideration should be given to the first two basic elements— the viewer position and the scene to be viewed.

Perceptually-based Management Recommendations

Our perceptually-based results support roadside mowing every three or four weeks when the grass becomes about 8 in. tall. Mowing should extend to some natural break close (within a couple mower widths) to the road's edge.

Annual maintenance and maintaining a 66% (or two-thirds) openness of vistas are equally preferred, so it would make sense to wait 5 to 7 years before trimming or cutting shrubs that would block distant views. Cutting that removes large amounts of woody vegetation from an overgrown vista is supported, but it is not supported when the vista is only partially blocked or when significant residual woody material would be left to partially block the view. In other words, we do not support cutting unless there is potential for creating substantial increased visual access or open views. Controlled burning is also not supported unless it shows potential for improvement in vista quality and extent.

Synthesis

The above summarized perceptual results regarding roadside mowing and vista maintenance speak for themselves. In addition, our analysis shows greater support for vista maintenance than for roadside mowing. The major synthesis would be the combination of periodic mowing of roadsides and brush clearing of vistas with introduction of native plant species that either (1) maintain low height and uniform texture or (2) are historically representative of past vegetation management practices at suitable locations. The latter would be especially appropriate near interpretive areas and facilities.

The question of the total mix of vegetative management over the length of the parkway is more difficult. Since our study dealt primarily with static images and simulations, we would propose that questions involving spatial sequences of visual experiences need sequential and dynamic simulation. One possibility for future research would be to simulate moving sequences of vegetative management changes along the Blue Ridge Parkway, utilizing video with different simulation media such as scale models, computer-assisted graphics, or electronic photomontage (computer and video) to illustrate different management alternatives in a "real time" sequence.

REFERENCES

Eastman-Kodak. 1981. *Making Color Prints with Kodak Ectaflex PCT Film and Paper*. New York: Eastman-Kodak Company.

Eastman-Kodak. 1982. *Using Your Kodak Ectaflex Printmaker Model 8*. New York: Eastman-Kodak Company.

Ilford, Inc. 1974. *Cibachrome Color Print Manual*. Ilford, Inc.

Ilford, Inc. 1983. *Retouching Cibachrome II Materials*. Technical Brochure TB34EN, Ilford, Inc.

Ilford, Inc. *Retouching Cibachrome Tips and Hints*. Ilford, Inc., undated.

Sheppard, S.R.J. 1979. The computer, the artist and the landscape architect. Presentation notes to the Bureau of Land Management Computer Graphics Workshop. Denver: The Conference.

Sheppard, S.R.J. 1982. Predictive landscape portrayals: a selective research review. *Landscape Journal* 1: 9–14.

Time-Life, Inc. 1981. *Photographer's Handbook Revised Edition*. New York Life Library of Photography, Time-Life Books, Inc.

U.S. Department of the Interior. 1980. Bureau of Land Management. *Visual Simulation*. Washington U.S. Government Printing Office.

Winer, B.J. 1971. *Statistical Principles in Experimental Design*. New York: McGraw-Hill Company.

Chapter Nine
Management Considerations

This chapter summarizes the major findings of the research reported in Chapters 2 through 8. Management considerations are also provided. The numbering of these management considerations does not indicate rank of importance.

Taken collectively, the findings form the basis for modifying the management covenants that establish guidelines for the development and maintenance practices along the Blue Ridge Parkway.

Chapter 2
(A Cognitive Psychological Approach)

Abstract

Sightseeing, a major outdoor recreational activity, depends greatly on the perceptions of visitors and the agency's management of the visual environment. To assist the Blue Ridge Parkway in managing its scenic landscapes, visitor preferences for parkway pull-off vistas were assessed, and options for managing the vegetation at vistas and roadsides were evaluated. Visual preference ratings of photographs were used to analyze the perception of Blue Ridge Parkway visitors for vista landscape scenes. A major purpose of the research sought to identify vista landscape themes or major landscape prototypes for developing a *visual preference typology* of vistas along the parkway.

This typology, based on those vista landscape themes most to least preferred, consists of scenes of (1) streams and rivers, (2) ponds and lakes, (3) mountains with several ridges, (4) pastoral development, (5) mountains with one ridge, and (6) unmaintained vegetation blocking the view. Among the management alternatives, the visitors favored the re-opening of vistas where vegetation blocks over 50% of the view and the mowing of only one mower width from the roadside.

Management Considerations

1. The Blue Ridge Parkway should continue to use visual preference ratings of on-site visitors in monitoring and managing the vistas and other visual resources of the parkway.
2. Based on the *visual preference typology* developed, the Blue Ridge Parkway should give priority to the management of those vistas most preferred by visitors.
3. An exception to the above category is the "unmaintained vegetation vistas." Re-opening of vistas where 50% or more of the view is blocked should receive priority, particularly if the vista landscape is a preferred type. However, visitors will tolerate vegetation blocking 20 to 30% of the view.
4. Roadside mowing should consist of one mower width (7 ft) from the road's edge, except in developed areas and around road or interpretive signs. Summer wildflowers should not be mowed when possible.

Chapter 3
(A Sociological Approach)

Abstract

The aesthetic preferences of 691 respondents were analyzed by using several relevant social background characteristics—socioeconomic status (SEI), age of respondent, sex of respondent, where the respondent was reared to age 16, highest educational level attained by the respondent, and the total household income of the respondent. The respondents were predominately male, equally likely to be raised in the city, town or country, highly educated, of higher occupational and income levels, and representative by age of the adult population in the United States. Individuals from lower social class levels were more likely to prefer the open vistas than those of the higher social class levels. Also, women were more likely than men to rate these vistas higher. Finally, older individuals rated these vistas higher than younger individuals.

Management Considerations

1. Given the "average" type of visitor to the parkway as represented in this sample, management should give serious consideration to the involvement of larger proportions of the visiting public. This presents a real problem that relates to the variety and complexity of vistas available for viewing. Perhaps more historical informa-

tion about the particular vistas and pull-offs can be made available for this visitor.

2. The vista preferred by most was the Water Vista. Access to these types of vistas could be further developed to serve as highlights of one's trip along the Blue Ridge.
3. The Open Vistas should be kept as a central and integral experience of the parkway visitor. Most aesthetic experiences of the average parkway user will be received from these vistas. A strategic concentration of resources on these pull-offs would have the maximum effect for an investment of resources.
4. Finally, and this consideration is related to no. 1, management of our aesthetic resources faces a real dilemma in trying to please all the users all the time. This is because the aesthetic preferences vary significantly by social class levels, age, and sex. This means that the diversity that presently exists in our parkways and parks needs to be preserved through continued democratic policy.

Chapter 4
(A Social Psychological Approach)

Abstract

The sightseeing experiences of the touring public were investigated by exploring how the tourists' attitudes and values toward recreation and the environment influence their scenic preferences. Differences in attitudes toward nature included a group that believed the environment should be exploited and developed, while another group believed in preserving and protecting the environment. Recreational values varied from those who were physically active to those who preferred passive activities such as sightseeing. In short, the tourists exhibited divergent interests toward scenic beauty depending on their environmental beliefs and recreational interests.

Management Considerations
1. The frequency of stopping at overlooks and pull-offs is considered an important indicator of interest for a sightseeing experience. About a third of the visiting public heavily used pull-offs and overlooks. These provided an opportunity for taking photographs, which is also an extension of the sightseeing experience. Obviously, maintenance of overlooks and pull-offs is important. The degree to which they are maintained can vary from completely open to partially obscured.
2. Another indicator of interest in the parkway experience is repeat visits. A significant number (about one-third) of the tourists return apparently to revisit park sites, again frequently stopping and

taking photographs to document their experience. This adds further support to continued maintenance of overlooks and pull-offs.

3. The majority of the tourists visiting the parkway believe that the aesthetic values associated with the roadway are important. Management should stress where the roadway offers visual opportunities through information and interpretive services.

4. The majority of tourists who believe that man must live in harmony with nature prefer the open vistas, but they also like the partially obscured vistas. Management can provide both forms of vistas but should realize that the open vista, irrespective of environmental attitudes, is preferred the most by the public.

5. The dominant recreational motive of experiencing the parkway through sightseeing activities, such as stopping and viewing, taking photographs, and learning through demonstration projects and interpretive programs, was central to the tourists' experience. This represents a highly passive recreational pattern adaptable to a parkway sightseeing experience. Programs reinforcing these passive recreational interests would be compatible with the interests of most of the parkway users.

6. Taste for open or maintained scenes also varied depending on the views tourists wish to see on the parkway. Those tourists who preferred to view natural scenes liked the open as well as the unmaintained vistas. Those tourists who preferred the rural pastoral scenes also liked the vistas that were open or just partially obscured. The maintenance of the parkway should be directed toward keeping vistas free of development and offering for view those aspects of nature and the rural visual experience which both tourist groups wish to experience.

Chapter 5
(A Psychophysical Approach)

Abstract
Enhancement of the scenic beauty of the landscape has long been a policy objective in the United States. However, the subjectivity involved in evaluating scenic beauty has hampered its incorporation into land management systems. In the first part of this chapter, the development of an approach to scenic beauty quantification is described. Based on the theory and methods of psychophysics, this approach derives metrics of perceived scenic beauty from observer ratings of photographic slides and then builds regression models of the scenic beauty metric predicted by observable and quantifiable landscape features. The second part of the chapter describes the application of this study on the Blue Ridge Parkway, in which the major research question concerned

the impact of foreground vegetation on scenic beauty. Foreground vegetation was found to influence the visitors' perceptions of scenic beauty, but the direction of the influence depended on the location of the vegetation in the visual field. A follow-up study explored alternative explanations of this locational effect and concluded that it was the result of photographic content rather than the observers' cognitive processes.

Management Considerations

1. Foreground vegetation is important to the visitors' perceptions of the scenic beauty of landscape vistas. Specific elements in the foreground vegetation may add to or detract from scenic beauty, but our research has not succeeded in identifying them. Therefore, we suggest reliance be placed on the expert judgments of landscape architects for minute vegetation management decisions on individual sites. Allocation by landscape architects can be based on estimates of visitation to the various vistas.

2. We have not studied the visual impacts of vegetation manipulation. For example, if controlled burns are used to eradicate unwanted woody plants, there may well be a severe, if temporary, reduction in overall scenic beauty. If mechanical means are used to reduce brushy vegetation, it is advisable to remove the cuttings since all research has demonstrated negative visual impacts from dead and down wood. Obviously, these suggestions must be interpreted in terms of other criteria in addition to scenic beauty. For example, if herbicides are used, visitors may object to what they see as poisoning of the environment. Considerations of cost, nutrient cycling, erosion control, and other factors may lead to a choice of management actions that are scenically non-optimal. If this is the case, managers are advised to provide interpretive programs that explain the necessity and temporary nature of the environmental disruption to the visitors.

3. A major conclusion from our research over the years is that visual effects do not increase or decrease steadily with changes in the physical environment. Instead, scenic beauty often behaves in a marginal utility manner, in which a small amount of damage, for example, causes rapid declines in perceived scenic beauty, after which additional damage has little negative effect. Therefore, it is possible that a small amount of vegetation management on certain vistas might significantly raise scenic beauty estimates, while expensive work at heavily overgrown sites may provide little improvement in visitor satisfaction. While we cannot be more specific in our suggestions, we would advise parkway management to inventory vista scenic resources to determine sites where investment in vegetation management might provide the greatest returns.

4. A final general suggestion emerging from our research is that in scenic beauty, one can have "too much of a good thing." As noted in Part I of our chapter, jagged mountains and large urban trees contribute to scenic beauty but apparently only up to some point, after which additional increments lead to declines in scenic beauty. As to foreground vegetation on the parkway, as a general rule the more open the vista the better. However, carried to an extreme, this management guideline might well be counter-productive. A certain amount of foreground vegetation provides vista framing or perhaps is attractive in itself, as with flowering shrubs or plants that attract birds. Lawn-like vista foregrounds might be viewed as unnatural, and this might become even more of a liability if preferences for unmodified nature increase in the future. Some mixture of enclosed and open vistas might be sought in an effort to promote landscape diversity, a quality generally regarded as central to enduring, quality visual experiences.

Chapter 6 (A Communications Approach)

Abstract

This chapter deals with the extent to which the images and preferences of landscapes held by people can be modified. Specifically, the effects of a message promoting values of unmowed roadsides on the visitors' preferences for photographs depicting mowed and unmowed scenes along the Blue Ridge Parkway were examined. Respondents exposed to brief interpretive messages promoting the value of infrequent mowing regimes exhibited little preference for high intensity mowing photographs. In contrast, use of the same interpretive message resulted in a greater acceptance of low intensity mowing photographs. The use of a message to affect a person's perception of mowing did not carry over to a person's perception of other vegetation management practices (e.g., burning, shrub removal or tree removal).

Management Considerations
1. Interpretation can be an effective tool for promoting public understanding and appreciation of management programs. For example, a message promoting the benefits of less mowing on the Blue Ridge Parkway can be used to change the expectation that the parkway will be maintained like a front lawn or golf course.
2. Interpretation can also be used to encourage desired visitor behaviors and to minimize behaviors inconsistent with management policies.
3. Interpretive messages can be developed to garner support and shape public opinion toward *specific* actions without being generalized to other management activities. For example, the reasons

for infrequent mowing regimes can be conveyed without visitors believing that other vegetation management practices (e.g., burning or tree removal) need to be reduced.
4. Positive images of Park Service operations can be developed. These images can be used to build constituent support, reduce unnecessary conflict, and produce better visitor understanding of National Park Service objectives.

Chapters 7 and 8
(Landscape Classification and
Landscape Management Approaches)

Abstract

Chapter 7 reviews the historic vegetative management practices of the Scot-Irish and German settlers, including girdling, cutting and burning, grazing, and natural selection. It also describes the development and application of a landscape classification system for the Blue Ridge landscape that is based primarily on physical form, spatial characteristics, and viewer interactions. It concludes with a description of the screening criteria used for selection of actual images for photomontage simulations and how representative these images are of the total sample of Blue Ridge scenes.

Chapter 8 documents how certain representative landscape scenes were selected and modified via photographic montage techniques to simulate proposed vegetative management alternatives. It then analyzes the respondents' scenic preferences for the visual simulations of the vegetation management alternatives. Management recommendations are presented for the maintenance of scenic overlooks and roadside areas based on the biophysical/historical analyses and the perceptual testing data.

Management Considerations

1. *Biophysical and Historical Management Considerations.* Because of a climate highly conducive to plant growth, potentially prime viewing sites require constant care. Consequently, the introduction of self-maintaining native plant species would have obvious advantages over species requiring labor-intensive management. Basically, candidate plants must favorably respond to the view and slope. Introduced perennial vegetation should respond to the following environmental characteristics. First, since most soils on steep slopes and ridges are thin and low in nutrients, plants should be shallow-rooted, fibrous, and able to absorb and hold nutrients for extended periods of time. Second, since the climate is temperate and humid and the rainfall abundant, plants should be able to withstand the potential erosive effects of heavy rainfall,

snow, and sedimentation. Plants should also be complementary in terms of form, size, and texture and respond to the surrounding site context; even more importantly, the height of the plant should be self-maintaining and predictable because placement on a given slope with respect to the viewer position is crucial in maintaining the desired view. In most cases, native grasses such as broom-sedge can be used. Again, consideration should be given to the first two basic elements—the viewer position and the scene to be viewed.

2. *Perceptually-based Management Considerations.* Perceptually-based results support roadside mowing every 3 or 4 weeks when the grass is about 8 in. tall. Mowing should extend to some natural break close (within a couple mower widths) to the road's edge. Annual maintenance and maintaining 66% openness of vistas are equally preferred, so shrub cutting should occur every 5 to 7 years when the shrubs begin to significantly block distant views. Cutting to remove large amounts of woody material from an over-grown vista is supported, but cutting is not supported when the vista is only partially blocked, or when significant residual woody material is left which partially blocks the view. In other words, we do not recommend cutting unless there is potential for creating substantial increased visual access or open views. Controlled burning is also not supported as a visual management technique unless it shows potential for substantial improvement in view vista quality and context.

3. *Synthesis.* The above recommendations regarding roadside mowing and vista maintenance speak for themselves. In addition, the analysis shows greater support for vista maintenance than roadside mowing. The major synthesis would be the combination of periodic mowing of roadsides and brush clearing combined with the introduction of native plants that either (1) maintain low height and uniform texture and/or (2) are historically representative of past vegetative management practices at suitable locations. The latter would be especially appropriate near interpretive areas and facilities.

The question of the total mix of vegetative management over the length of the parkway is more difficult. Since the investigators dealt primarily with static images and simulations, we would propose that questions involving spatial sequences of visual experiences need sequential or dynamic simulation. Future research could simulate moving sequences of vegetative management changes along the Blue Ridge Parkway, utilizing video with different simulation media such as scale models, computer-assisted graphics, or electric photomontage (computer and video) to illustrate management alternatives in "real time" sequence.

Conclusions

At the time of printing, the data base gathered from this multi-disciplinary research project was still in the process of being further analyzed. The contributors to this book only dealt with the broad findings and trends. More specific theoretical and methodological issues will be published in scientific journals.

Understanding visual preference still remains an area of study where few explanations are available, but it is of great interest to those agencies and institutions that offer sightseeing experiences. We trust that the different approaches presented in this monograph give the reader an expanded outlook toward the many complexities associated with the issue of measuring visual preference.

Appendix A

Questionnaire used for the vista preference study, 1982. Data from this questionnaire were used to fulfill the objectives of the research described in Chapters 2 through 4.

VISUAL PREFERENCE STUDY

A Visual Survey of Blue Ridge Parkway Overlooks

The University of Tennessee, with permission from the Blue Ridge
Parkway, is researching what visitors like to see at Parkway overlooks.
Your ratings of the photographs, plus your answers to the additional
questions, will aid the National Park Service in the management and
planning of the Blue Ridge Parkway.

Instructions

First, please look through the pictures quickly to get a general
feeling for what they are about. Then, go back and RATE EACH OF THE
SCENES AS TO HOW MUCH YOU LIKE IT.

All you need to do is circle the number below EACH photograph to
indicate whether you like the scene:


```
1 = not at all

2 = a little

3 = somewhat

4 = quite a bit

5 = very much
```


THANK YOU

Donald G. Hodges
The University of Tennessee

1 2 3 4 5   1 2 3 4 5

1 2 3 4 5   1 2 3 4 5

1 2 3 4 5   1 2 3 4 5

1 2 3 4 5   1 2 3 4 5

1 2 3 4 5   1 2 3 4 5

1 2 3 4 5   1 2 3 4 5

1 2 3 4 5   1 2 3 4 5

1 2 3 4 5   1 2 3 4 5

1 2 3 4 5

1 2 3 4 5

1 2 3 4 5

1 2 3 4 5

1 2 3 4 5

1 2 3 4 5

1 2 3 4 5

1 2 3 4 5

1 2 3 4 5

1 2 3 4 5

1 2 3 4 5

1 2 3 4 5

1 2 3 4 5

1 2 3 4 5

1 2 3 4 5

1 2 3 4 5

To better understand your ratings of the photographs, we need to know something of your current trip, and any past trips, on the Blue Ridge Parkway. Would you please answer the following questions?

CURRENT TRIP

1. How many <u>days</u>, or what part of a day, did you spend traveling along the Blue Ridge Parkway on your current trip? _____ DAY(S)

2. Approximately how many miles is it from your current residence to the point at which you <u>entered</u> the Blue Ridge Parkway? _____ MILES

3. On this trip, was the Blue Ridge Parkway: (check most appropriate answer)

   _____ YOUR MAJOR DESTINATION
   _____ ONE OF TWO OR THREE MAJOR DESTINATIONS
   _____ ONE OF MANY DESTINATIONS
   _____ NOT A DESTINATION

4. What other natural areas did you visit during <u>this</u> trip? (check as many as apply to your visit)

   _____ SHENANDOAH NATIONAL PARK
   _____ GREAT SMOKY MOUNTAINS NATIONAL PARK
   _____ NATIONAL FORESTS
   _____ STATE PARKS OR FORESTS
   _____ OTHER (please specify) _____

   _____ I DID NOT VISIT ANY OTHER NATURAL AREAS ON THIS TRIP.

5. People have many reasons for traveling the Blue Ridge Parkway. A number of these reasons are listed below. Please indicate how important <u>you</u> feel <u>each</u> reason is for your use of the Parkway on this visit.

	Not at all Important	Somewhat Important	Important	Very Important	Extremely Important	Does Not Apply
a. to visit relative or friends	( )	( )	( )	( )	( )	( )
b. to go to and from work	( )	( )	( )	( )	( )	( )
c. to take a vacation	( )	( )	( )	( )	( )	( )
d. to view the scenery along the Parkway	( )	( )	( )	( )	( )	( )
e. to participate in outdoor recreational activities such as camping, hiking, picnicking, etc.	( )	( )	( )	( )	( )	( )
f. to visit Parkway facilities such as visitor centers, demonstration areas, etc.	( )	( )	( )	( )	( )	( )
g. to learn more about the area	( )	( )	( )	( )	( )	( )
h. Other (specify)_____	( )	( )	( )	( )	( )	( )

6. On this trip: (please circle best approximation)

   a. how many pull-off overlooks did you stop at?

      0   1-2   3-5   6-10   11-15   15+

   b. how many pictures did you take at pull-off overlooks

      0   1-5   6-10   11-20   21-36   36+

7. Many factors may influence why you stop or do not stop at a given overlook. Please indicate whether each of the following encouraged or dis-
   couraged you from stopping at the overlooks.

		Greatly Discouraged	Mildly Discouraged	No Effect	Mildly Encouraged	Greatly Encouraged	Did not en- counter factor
a.	Pull off was on your side of road	( )	( )	( )	( )	( )	( )
b.	Overlook not well main-tained	( )	( )	( )	( )	( )	( )
c.	Information sign at over-look	( )	( )	( )	( )	( )	( )
d.	Had already stopped at a similar overlook	( )	( )	( )	( )	( )	( )
e.	Trail starting at over-look	( )	( )	( )	( )	( )	( )
f.	View from overlook	( )	( )	( )	( )	( )	( )
g.	Shrubs or trees blocking view	( )	( )	( )	( )	( )	( )
h.	Rock information at overlook	( )	( )	( )	( )	( )	( )
i.	Had to drive extra $\frac{1}{2}$-$\frac{1}{4}$ mile off Parkway to overlook	( )	( )	( )	( )	( )	( )
j.	Stream at pull off	( )	( )	( )	( )	( )	( )
k.	Other cars stopped at overlook	( )	( )	( )	( )	( )	( )
l.	Picnic site at overlook	( )	( )	( )	( )	( )	( )
m.	exhibit at overlook	( )	( )	( )	( )	( )	( )
n.	Good subject for photo-graphy	( )	( )	( )	( )	( )	( )
o.	Other (specify)_____	( )	( )	( )	( )	( )	( )

8. At different points along the Parkway, there are numerous facilities pro-
    vided for you and other visitors. Please indicate how important each of
    the following is to your enjoyment of the Blue Ridge Parkway. (please
    check each item)

		Not at all Important	Somewhat Important	Important	Very Important	Extremely Important
a.	bathrooms	( )	( )	( )	( )	( )
b.	picnic tables	( )	( )	( )	( )	( )
c.	information signs	( )	( )	( )	( )	( )
d.	parking space	( )	( )	( )	( )	( )
e.	trash containers	( )	( )	( )	( )	( )
f.	drinking water	( )	( )	( )	( )	( )
g.	pamphlets	( )	( )	( )	( )	( )
h.	nature trails	( )	( )	( )	( )	( )
i.	Parkway exhibits	( )	( )	( )	( )	( )
j.	maps	( )	( )	( )	( )	( )
k.	hiking trails	( )	( )	( )	( )	( )
l.	other _____	( )	( )	( )	( )	( )

9. When you stop at Parkway pulloffs or overlooks: how frequently do you
    do each of the following (please check each item).

		Never	Seldom	Occasion-ally	Fre-quently	Almost Always
a.	get out of the car	( )	( )	( )	( )	( )
b.	read information signs	( )	( )	( )	( )	( )
c.	take photographs	( )	( )	( )	( )	( )
d.	discuss what you see with those in your group	( )	( )	( )	( )	( )
e.	picnic	( )	( )	( )	( )	( )
f.	hike	( )	( )	( )	( )	( )
g.	talk to others stopped at pulloff	( )	( )	( )	( )	( )
h.	explore the area	( )	( )	( )	( )	( )
i.	try to identify what you see	( )	( )	( )	( )	( )
j.	other _____	( )	( )	( )	( )	( )

10. While driving along the Parkway, how frequently do you engage in the following activities. (please check each item)

	Never	Seldom	Occasionally	Frequently	Almost Always
a. talk about what you see	( )	( )	( )	( )	( )
b. point out items of interest	( )	( )	( )	( )	( )
c. have one person act as guide	( )	( )	( )	( )	( )
d. take photographs from your vehicle	( )	( )	( )	( )	( )
e. use a guidebook of the Parkway	( )	( )	( )	( )	( )
f. remain silent as you view the Parkway	( )	( )	( )	( )	( )
g. carry on conversations not related to Parkway	( )	( )	( )	( )	( )
h. other _____	( )	( )	( )	( )	( )

11. Do you feel that you have to stop and get out of your vehicle to enjoy the scenery along the Parkway? (please check most appropriate answer)

_____ YES, USUALLY

_____ YES, SOMETIMES

_____ UNDECIDED

_____ NO, NOT USUALLY

_____ NO, NOT AT ALL

12. Considering the number of pulloffs that you typically stop at, how would reducing the number of pulloffs affect your enjoyment of the Parkway? (please check most appropriate answer)

_____ IT WOULD REDUCE MY ENJOYMENT A GREAT DEAL

_____ IT WOULD REDUCE MY ENJOYMENT SOMEWHAT

_____ IT WOULD NOT AFFECT MY ENJOYMENT

_____ UNDECIDED

13. The Blue Ridge Parkway has a large variety of scenery. A number of
     these different scenes are listed below. For each one, check the box
     that indicates how desirable you feel each type of scenery is:

		Not at all	Neutral	A little	Somewhat	Quite a bit	Very much
a.	small towns or communities	( )	( )	( )	( )	( )	( )
b.	mountain peaks and ridges	( )	( )	( )	( )	( )	( )
c.	rivers flowing through farms	( )	( )	( )	( )	( )	( )
d.	distant views of flat plains	( )	( )	( )	( )	( )	( )
e.	rolling hills	( )	( )	( )	( )	( )	( )
f.	flowering plants	( )	( )	( )	( )	( )	( )
g.	valleys	( )	( )	( )	( )	( )	( )
h.	tall trees	( )	( )	( )	( )	( )	( )
i.	steep dropoffs or cliffs	( )	( )	( )	( )	( )	( )
j.	farms and farm buildings	( )	( )	( )	( )	( )	( )
k.	other _____	( )	( )	( )	( )	( )	( )

PAST USE

1. How many different years have you visited the Blue Ridge Parkway? (For
    example if you visited the Parkway in 1968, 1980, and this year your
    answer would be 3 years). _____ YEARS

2. Other than this trip, how many times have you visited the Parkway during...

    the last year?   _____ NUMBER OF TRIPS

    the last 5 years?   _____ NUMBER OF TRIPS

    the last 10 years?   _____ NUMBER OF TRIPS

3. On the average about how many days per trip do you spend on the Blue Ridge
    Parkway? _____ DAYS/TRIP

USER INFORMATION

These questions deal with information that will help us determine the future use of the Blue Ridge Parkway. All information is striclty confidential and will not be associated with you as an individual.

1. Current residence:_____
                                    city   state

2. What is your occupation? Please be as specific as possible, tell what kind of work you do, not for whom you work. If student, housewife, or retired, please say so. _____

3. In what <u>year</u> were you born? _____

4. Sex: _____ MALE
        _____ FEMALE

5. Check the box that best describes where you lived most of the time before your 16th birthday.

   _____ on a farm or ranch
   _____ in the country but not on a farm or ranch
   _____ in a small town (population less than 2,500)
   _____ in a town or small city (2,501 - 25,000)
   _____ in a city (25,001 - 100,000)
   _____ in a suburb and within 25 miles of a large city (more than 100,000)
   _____ in a large city (more than 100,000)

6. Education: check the <u>highest</u> level attained

   _____ 8th grade or less
   _____ Attended high school
   _____ Graduated from high school
   _____ Technical/Business school
   _____ Attended college
   _____ Completed college
   _____ Advanced degree

7. Income: check the level that contains your 1981 <u>TOTAL FAMILY INCOME</u> before taxes.

   _____ LESS THAN $5,000
   _____ $5,000 - $9,999
   _____ $10,000 - 14,999
   _____ $15,000 - 19,999
   _____ $20,000 - 29,999
   _____ $30,000 - 39,999
   _____ $40,000+

Up to this point the questions have dealt directly with your trip to the Blue Ridge Parkway. Now we would like to ask a few more general questions about some environmental and group related attitudes which may be important to this study. We would appreciate you giving us your opinion on these items.

ENVIRONMENTAL ISSUES-OPINIONS

We would like to get your opinion on a wide range of environmental issues. For each of the following statements, please indicate the extent to which you agree or disagree by checking the appropriate box.

	Strongly Agree	Somewhat Agree	Neutral	Somewhat Disagree	Strongly Disagree	Don't Know
1. We are approaching the limit of the number of people the earth can support.	( )	( )	( )	( )	( )	( )
2. The balance of nature is very delicate and easily upset.	( )	( )	( )	( )	( )	( )
3. Most citizens are concerned about the quality of the environment.	( )	( )	( )	( )	( )	( )
4. Humans have the right to modify the natural environment to suit their needs.	( )	( )	( )	( )	( )	( )
5. Mankind was created to rule over the rest of nature.	( )	( )	( )	( )	( )	( )
6. The roadside is a reflection of a vitality which is typically American.	( )	( )	( )	( )	( )	( )
7. When humans interfere with nature it often produces disastrous consequences.	( )	( )	( )	( )	( )	( )
8. Plants and animals exist primarily to be used by humans.	( )	( )	( )	( )	( )	( )
9. The average citizen can exercise a good deal of control over the characteristics of the physical environment.	( )	( )	( )	( )	( )	( )
10. To maintain a healthy economy, we will have to develop a "steady-state" economy where industrial growth is controlled.	( )	( )	( )	( )	( )	( )
11. Humans must live in harmony with nature in order to survive.	( )	( )	( )	( )	( )	( )

12. Highways are meaningful and inviting, not just a way of getting to some place. ( ) ( ) ( ) ( ) ( ) ( )

13. The earth is like a space ship with only limited room and resources. ( ) ( ) ( ) ( ) ( ) ( )

14. Humans need not adapt to the natural environment because they can re-make it to suit their needs. ( ) ( ) ( ) ( ) ( ) ( )

----

15. Changing woodlands and fields by landscaping, trimming, and cutting spoils nature's beauty. ( ) ( ) ( ) ( ) ( ) ( )

16. There are limits to growth beyond which our industrialized society cannot expand. ( ) ( ) ( ) ( ) ( ) ( )

17. Mankind is severely abusing the environment. ( ) ( ) ( ) ( ) ( ) ( )

18. Most everything along a highway looks the same. ( ) ( ) ( ) ( ) ( ) ( )

GROUPS AND OUTDOOR RECREATION ATTITUDES

1. How many people, besides yourself, accompanied you while traveling the Parkway on your current trip? _____ PEOPLE

2. What is your relationship to the majority of this traveling group? (check most appropriate item)

    _____ HUSBAND
    _____ WIFE
    _____ SON
    _____ DAUGHTER
    _____ FRIEND
    _____ OTHER (please specify) _____

3. On your Parkway trip, what type of group did you travel with? (check one)

    _____ ALONE
    _____ FRIENDS
    _____ AN ORGANIZED GROUP
    _____ FAMILY
    _____ BOTH FAMILY AND FRIENDS
    _____ OTHER (please specify)_____

If you checked 'FAMILY' or 'FAMILY AND FRIENDS' on question 3 (previous page) please answer these remaining three questions. If you checked any of the other answers you are finished with the questionnaire.

4. What kinds of outdoor recreational activities do you and your family do together most frequently? _____
    _____

    a. Of those activities just mentioned (if any), which <u>one</u> do you and your family do most frequently? _____

    b. How often do you do this activity? _____ TIMES PER YEAR

    c. Who usually decides to do this activity?

        _____ HUSBAND ONLY

        _____ WIFE ONLY

        _____ HUSBAND AND WIFE ONLY

        _____ CHILDREN ONLY

        _____ ALL FAMILY MEMBERS

        _____ OTHER (specify) _____

5. Which of the following statements best describes how you feel about recreational activities that you and your family may do together?

    _____ I receive more enjoyment from recreational activities when I do them alone.

    _____ I receive about the same amount of enjoyment from recreational activities whether I do them alone or with my family.

    _____ I receive more enjoyment from recreational activities when I do them with my family.

6. For __each__ statement below please check the box that best describes your
    opinion of the statement.

	Strongly Disagree	Disagree	Neutral	Agree	Strongly Agree
a. I think my family should do more things together.	( )	( )	( )	( )	( )
b. I feel that as a family, we are able to do most things together as well as other families do.	( )	( )	( )	( )	( )
c. I feel that as a family, we do not enjoy things together as much as other families do.	( )	( )	( )	( )	( )
d. I feel that my family has only a little of which to be proud.	( )	( )	( )	( )	( )
e. I feel that my family is on an equal level of most other families in terms of doing things together.	( )	( )	( )	( )	( )
f. The members of my family usually have a postive attitude toward each other.	( )	( )	( )	( )	( )
g. On the whole, I find that the activities I do with the members of my family to be enjoyable.	( )	( )	( )	( )	( )

THANK YOU

Appendix B

Questionnaire used for the vegetation management preference study, 1983. Data from this questionnaire were used to fulfill the objectives of the research described in chapters 5 through 8.

VISUAL PREFERENCES ALONG A SCENIC PARKWAY
Perceptions of Vegetation Management

Vegetation management along the Blue Ridge Parkway can be conducted at various levels of intensity. For example, the roadside grass can be mowed weekly, monthly, bi-monthly, etc. We would like your opinion to some possible levels of grass mowing and tree clearing that might be practiced on the Parkway. By rating the vegetation management examples in our photos, we can determine what Parkway visitors prefer.

Instruction

There is a collection of photographs presented as three (3) pairs per page.

EXAMPLE:

Each picture has a short description under it. Please pay particular attention to the described feature as you rate each photograph.

First, look through them quickly to get a general feeling for the photographs. Then, go back and carefully read the description. Rate EACH photo (compared to its pair) for HOW MUCH YOU LIKE IT. Simply circle the number of your choice below each photograph.

```
1 = not at all
2 = a little
3 = somewhat
4 = quite a bit
5 = very much
```

Thank you!

Kathlyne A. McGee
The University of Tennessee

"There are idle spots on every farm-
and every highway is bordered by an idle strip as long as it is.
Keep cow, plow, and mower out of these idle spots, and the full
native flora, plus dozens of
interesting stowaways
could be part of the normal
environment of every citizen."

Aldo Leopold,
Pioneer Ecologist

from

A Sand County Almanac

Just a 50% reduction
in mowing on the
Blue Ridge Parkway
will save taxpayers $71,000 per year.

There is an economy in natural things.

1a   **1b**

1   2   3   4   5   No mowing beyond
guardrail.

1   2   3   4   5   Mowing to and beyond guardrail.

2a   **2b**

1   2   3   4   5   Mowed one mower
width from roadside.

1   2   3   4   5   Mowed to treeline.

3a   **3b**

1   2   3   4   5   No mowing.

1   2   3   4   5   Complete
mowing into treeline.

4a   **4b**

1 2 3 4 5 Vegetation not
mowed around sign.

1 2 3 4 5 Vegetation mowed
around & beyond sign.

5a   **5b**

1 2 3 4 5 Shrub vegetation
in near foreground.

1 2 3 4 5 Shrubs managed by
controlled burning.

6a   **6b**

1 2 3 4 5 Mowed one mower
width from roadside.

1 2 3 4 5 Mowing complete to
treeline.

 **7a**

1 2 3 4 5 Mowing to treeline.

7b

1 2 3 4 5 Mowed one mower
width from roadside.

 **8a**

1 2 3 4 5 Mowed only at
mid-summer.

8b

1 2 3 4 5 Mowed every
three weeks.

 **9a**

1 2 3 4 5 Only roadside
shoulder mowed.

9b

1 2 3 4 5 Mowed to fenceline
and beyond.

 **10a 10b**

1 2 3 4 5 Trees closing in
the scenic vista.

1 2 3 4 5 Low shrubs in
distant foreground.

 **11a 11b**

1 2 3 4 5 Vista with some
trees in foreground.

1 2 3 4 5 Trees removed from
foreground in vista.

 **12a 12b**

1 2 3 4 5 Foreground trees
in vista.

1 2 3 4 5 No foreground trees
in vista.

13a 13b

1 2 3 4 5 Scene with foreground trees.

1 2 3 4 5 Foreground trees
completely removed.

14a 14 b

1 2 3 4 5 Hardwood and
conifer (evergreen) trees present.

1 2 3 4 5 Hardwoods cut to
emphasize conifers.

15a 15b

1 2 3 4 5 Shrubs in
foreground.

1 2 3 4 5 Shrubs removed by
cutting & controlled burning.

 **16a 16b**

1 2 3 4 5 Trees closing in
vista more than 50%.

1 2 3 4 5 Selective cutting
to re-open vista.

 **17a 17b**

1 2 3 4 5 Low shrubs in
distant foreground.

1 2 3 4 5 Mowing and cutting
of foreground vegetation.

 **18a 18b**

1 2 3 4 5 Original scene
with edge trees.

1 2 3 4 5 Single edge tree
removed.

THANK YOU for rating the photos. We now have a few questions for you to answer which will help us interpret your ratings and leisure patterns.

VEGETATION MANAGEMENT ALTERNATIVES

The following items describe various levels at which the grass and shrubs along the Blue Ridge Parkway could be maintained. Please indicate whether you support or do not support each of the following management options. (Circle the most appropriate response for each statement).

		Strongly Support	Support	Probably Support	Don't Know	Probably Don't Support	Don't Support	Definitely Don't Support
I.	The roadside grass should be mowed:							
1.	weekly, like a lawn.	1	2	3	4	5	6	7
2.	every two weeks, when 3 to 6 inches tall.	1	2	3	4	5	6	7
3.	once per month, when at least 10 inches tall.	1	2	3	4	5	6	7
4.	once in the Fall after the wildflowers are through blooming.	1	2	3	4	5	6	7
5.	only one mower width (7 feet) from the edge of the road surface.	1	2	3	4	5	6	7
6.	two mower widths (14 feet) from the road's edge.	1	2	3	4	5	6	7
7.	from the road's edge to the ditch or swale.	1	2	3	4	5	6	7
8.	from the road's edge to the treeline.	1	2	3	4	5	6	7
9.	as little as possible, only when necessary to maintain driver safety and help prevent grass fires.	1	2	3	4	5	6	7
II.	Shrubs and trees at pull-off vistas should be cut or trimmed:							
10.	annually to maintain a completely clear view.	1	2	3	4	5	6	7
11.	every 5 to 7 years, before the shrubs in the foreground block much of the distant view.	1	2	3	4	5	6	7
12.	just often enough so that no more than 1/3 of the view is blocked.	1	2	3	4	5	6	7

OUTDOOR ACTIVITIES

We would like to ask some questions about the kind of outdoor recreation activities in which you participate. FIRST, place a check mark only by those activities in which you annually participate, AND SECONDLY, indicate how often you do these activities by circling the appropriate code number.

Code
1	1 wk+	=	Once a week or more
2	2-3 mth	=	Two to three times a month
3	1 mth	=	Once a month
4	1 cple mth	=	Once every couple months
5	2-3 yr	=	Two to three times a year
6	1 yr	=	Once a year

		1 wk+	2-3 mth	1 mth	1 cple mth	2-3 yr	1 yr
1.	_____ Camping in remote wilderness areas	1	2	3	4	5	6
2.	_____ Camping in developed campgrounds	1	2	3	4	5	6
3.	_____ Hunting	1	2	3	4	5	6
4.	_____ Fishing	1	2	3	4	5	6
5.	_____ Riding motorcycles, trailmobiles, snowmobiles, etc. off the road	1	2	3	4	5	6
6.	_____ Driving 4-wheel drive vehicles off the road	1	2	3	4	5	6
7.	_____ Wildlife and bird photography	1	2	3	4	5	6
8.	_____ Bird watching	1	2	3	4	5	6
9.	_____ Hiking	1	2	3	4	5	6
10.	_____ Nature walks	1	2	3	4	5	6
11.	_____ Walking for pleasure	1	2	3	4	5	6
12.	_____ Bicycling	1	2	3	4	5	6
13.	_____ Horseback riding	1	2	3	4	5	6
14.	_____ Canoeing	1	2	3	4	5	6
15.	_____ Sailing	1	2	3	4	5	6
16.	_____ Other boating (water skiing)	1	2	3	4	5	6
17.	_____ Outdoor pool swimming	1	2	3	4	5	6
18.	_____ Other swimming outdoors	1	2	3	4	5	6
19.	_____ Golf	1	2	3	4	5	6
20.	_____ Tennis	1	2	3	4	5	6

		1 wk+	2-3 mth	1 mth	1 cple mt,	2-3 yr	1 yr
21.	_____ Playing other outdoor games or sports	1	2	3	4	5	6
22.	_____ Going to outdoor concerts, plays	1	2	3	4	5	6
23.	_____ Going to outdoor sports events	1	2	3	4	5	6
24.	_____ Visiting zoos, fairs, amusement parks	1	2	3	4	5	6
25.	_____ Sightseeing	1	2	3	4	5	6
26.	_____ Picnicking	1	2	3	4	5	6
27.	_____ Driving for pleasure	1	2	3	4	5	6
28.	_____ Other outdoor activities (please specify) _____	1	2	3	4	5	6

Do you attend

		1 wk+	2-3 mth	1 mth	1 cple mt,	2-3 yr	1 yr
29.	_____ Football games	1	2	3	4	5	6
30.	_____ Basketball games	1	2	3	4	5	6
31.	_____ Baseball games	1	2	3	4	5	6
32.	_____ Track and field	1	2	3	4	5	6
33.	_____ Other _____	1	2	3	4	5	6
34.	_____ How often do you watch sports on TV?	1	2	3	4	5	6

LEISURE ATTITUDES

These items measure your attitudes toward leisure. By this we mean how you feel about your leisure, your recreation, or the things you do in your free time. Please answer as quickly and accurately as possible indicating whether you agree or disagree with each of the following statements. (Circle the appropriate response for each statement).

	Strongly Agree	Agree	Probably Agree	Don't Know	Probably Disagree	Disagree	Strongly Disagree
1. Leisure is my most enjoyable time.	1	2	3	4	5	6	7
2. I admire a person who knows how to relax.	1	2	3	4	5	6	7
3. I like to do things on the spur of the moment.	1	2	3	4	5	6	7
4. I would like to lead a life of complete leisure.	1	2	3	4	5	6	7
5. Most people spend too much time enjoying themselves today.	1	2	3	4	5	6	7
6. I don't feel guilty about enjoying myself.	1	2	3	4	5	6	7
7. People should seek as much leisure as possible in their lives.	1	2	3	4	5	6	7
8. I'd like to have at least two months vacation a year.	1	2	3	4	5	6	7
9. Leisure is great.	1	2	3	4	5	6	7
10. It is good for adults to be playful.	1	2	3	4	5	6	7

Index